Asking Questions About Behavior

An Introduction to What Psychologists Do

Asking Questions About Behavior

An Introduction to What Psychologists Do

Michael E. Doherty and
Kenneth M. Shemberg
Bowling Green State University

Scott, Foresman and Company

Library of Congress Catalog Card No. 74-109234

Copyright © 1970 by Scott, Foresman and Company,
Glenview, Illinois 60025.
Philippines Copyright 1970 by Scott, Foresman and Company.
All Rights Reserved. Printed in the United States of America.

Regional offices of Scott, Foresman and Company are located in Atlanta, Dallas, Glenview, Palo Alto, Oakland, N.J., and London, England.

Preface

Every year students sign up for an introductory psychology course eagerly hoping to find out why they feel and act as they do and what makes other people tick. They expect psychology to help them to be more effective, happier people, to make the best use of their potential. They also hope to understand something of the murky depths of unconscious and irrational forces on their attitudes and behaviors. Long before the end of the term many of these students are disappointed, disillusioned, looking elsewhere for the answers to *real-life* questions that they had hoped psychology could give them. They see no earthly reason for learning about reflex arcs and standard deviations and the behavior of rats and pigeons. They feel cheated, and most of them never take another course in psychology, seeing psychology evermore as a hodgepodge of irrelevant and trivial facts.

It is our belief that such disillusionment is unnecessary. Professional psychologists are so inured to the need for careful controls and for asking answerable questions that they assume such needs are self-evident, forgetting the circuitous paths and painful stages by which they themselves came to hold their convictions and enthusiasms. We have become convinced that what we need to do with our beginning students is show them what happens when one starts to study relevant questions, taking them over the bridge from the lively concerns *they* bring to the questions psychologists can ask and get meaningful answers to. So in this book we start with one of the questions many students bring to an introductory course and show what happens when we try to answer it.

Part I begins the quest, with a list of questions such as students ask on the first day of class, and one of these—"Why does one's personality change when under stress?"—is picked out and analyzed word by word to show that it is unanswerable—and why—and the requirements of an answerable question are examined.

Part II then recounts nine diverse research studies, each directed at one aspect of the relationship between stress and personality. These accounts show how research using different designs and different kinds of subjects can tackle different aspects and build a cumulative, ever more comprehensive picture. Included are studies of Freudian hypotheses concerning childhood stress, Brady's study of ulcers in "executive" monkeys, Schachter's work on the relationship between stress and the tendency to seek closeness to other people, Miller's classic study demonstrating the motive power of learned fear, the investigation by Hebb and others of effects of sensory deprivation and isolation, Masserman's work with experimental neuroses in animals, Johnson's study of the role of physiological arousal in experimental neuroses, Cannon's fascinating attempt to analyze the mechanisms responsible for voodoo deaths, and a case of a severely disturbed boy in whom glasses-wearing behavior was established and tantrum behavior was extinguished by "behavior modification" techniques. The stories of how and why these studies were carried out are told in narrative, nontechnical style, and in each case we try to point out both what was demonstrated and what questions were *not* answered by the study.

Finally, in Part III, based on the preceding examples, we are ready to draw some generalizations concerning control, research strategies, replication, quantification, sources of research questions, and ethical considerations. We also introduce briefly two main approaches exemplified in the studies described earlier, and in the field today: the *theoretical* approach, utilizing constructs and explicit theoretical assumptions, and the *atheoretical* approach of attempting to limit oneself to relationships between oberservable phenomena.

Starting out in pursuit of answers that students would like to have to questions of deep and real concern to them, we thus have tried to lead them back, step by step, to see and appreciate the precision of questioning that is needed for meaningful research. They will find that one question leads to another, that before they can pin down one facet they need to specify certain others. It is our hope that in the end they will even see why reflex arcs and standard deviations and findings about rats and pigeons can be important, and how and why grown men and women can get so excited about them. Perhaps they will even share some of the excitement themselves.

Contents

Part I *Asking Questions*

Introduction — 2
Asking Important Questions — 3
Asking Answerable Questions — 5

Part II *Some Answers*

Childhood Stress and Adult Personality — 15
One Effect of Stress On the Body — 21
Stress and Affiliation — 25
Stress and Learning — 31
The Effect of Profound Isolation on Personality — 36
Experimental Neurosis — 43
A Psychophysiological Approach to Stress — 51
Voodoo Death — 58
Behavior Modification — 63
Brief Descriptions of Other Studies of Stress and Personality — 73

Part III *Conclusions*

Some Principles of Research — 78
   Control — 78
   Research Strategies — 83
   Replication — 87
   Quantification — 89
   Where Do Questions Come From? — 94
   Ethics — 97
Considerations Which May Determine Future Questions — 99
   Interrelatedness of Questions — 100
   Why Theory? — 103
   An Alternative Point of View — 105
   Which Approach Is Better? — 108
   Concluding Remarks — 109

References — 111

Part I

Asking Questions

INTRODUCTION

Introductory psychology textbooks have almost universally adopted an inductive model with which to present the data and theory of the science of psychology. Briefly, this means that the texts typically progress from specific to more general topics. The basic assumption underlying this progression is that the more complex areas of study in psychology like personality and social psychology can be understood in terms of simpler processes like learning, motivation, and perception. Thus, the reasoning goes, only if the student first comprehends the laws governing the elements, will he be able to understand the more complex aspects of behavior.

There are, to be sure, many good reasons for writing beginning psychology textbooks in this fashion. However, the present authors believe that there is one respect in which the presentation of psychology in the usual inductive pattern is unfortunate. While such a presentation organizes the data in a logically and psychologically meaningful way, the inductive approach does not truly reflect what a psychologist *does*. Presenting psychology inductively is likely to leave the reader with an inaccurate picture of the relative maturity of psychology as a scientific discipline. Putting this another way, the inductive approach is likely to leave the reader with a false impression of the extent to which the goals of the science of psychology are clearly defined. It would be well for the student of psychology to know at the very outset of his studies that the science of psychology is very young and that its goals are presently ill-defined.

Not too long ago psychologists were attempting to develop theories which were very broad and which would enable one to explain all aspects of behavior. Some psychologists are now engaged in the development of smaller, less grand theories to explain much more limited aspects of behavior. Others are not seeking to develop theories at all. Now, virtually all research psychologists have abandoned the pursuit of the Holy

Grail of grand behavior theory. We might be interested in the totality of behavior, and we would like to understand the totality of behavior. But the impossibility of doing so at this point in time is forced upon us by the fantastic complexity of the interrelationships between the environment and the organism. There are literally billions of events occurring at any given moment in time within the organism and at the point of contact between the organism and the environment. So psychological researchers often devote themselves to one of the "simpler" phenomena such as learning, motivation, or perception. But these, too, are incredibly complicated, and the body of data available from the research studies that relate to any one of them staggers the imagination. So in actual practice a psychologist studies intensively some small aspect of one of the so-called simpler behavioral phenomena, in the hope that he will discover the knowledge necessary to understand some small piece of the environment-organism interaction. There is as yet no Einstein on the horizon of scientific psychology who is promising to construct the psychological counterpart of relativity theory!

If contemporary psychologists are not attempting to construct all-inclusive, broad theories of behavior, what are they doing? What is the goal which provides the motivation for the many studies you will find sprinkled liberally throughout your text? That is the question to which the present book is addressed. Why do psychologists do the kinds of things they do? Why do they ask the kinds of questions they ask? Why does one ask, for example, Will depriving a very young rat of food affect his later behavior? when you, the student, have so many seemingly more interesting and important questions you'd like to have answered?

ASKING IMPORTANT QUESTIONS

How much influence does environment have on personality development?

Can a chemical imbalance in one's system affect the unconscious mind, and if so, can it be detected through behavior?

What possesses a person to act like an authority about a subject even though he may know nothing about the subject?

How much influence do parents actually have on their children's ideas of life?

Why are people prejudiced toward other people?

Why do people purposefully humiliate and physically harm their loved ones, even though they are aware of the emotional and bodily harm that results from their actions?

Why is something a fear stimulus for one person and not another?

What are the psychological "causes" or theories for the development of a subculture such as a juvenile gang or a street-corner society?

What are the determining factors which make up a "stable" person and what are the limits to stability?

What causes some people to become very hot-headed and blow up into a temper tantrum?

Why does one's personality change when under stress?

The above are some of the replies given by students on the first day of a class in introductory psychology when asked what question about human behavior they would most like answered by a course in psychology. These are all "good" questions, some dealing with issues of great personal relevance, others with issues of overbearing social importance. It is very possible that the reader is beginning this course in psychology with similar questions. It is also quite possible that neither the questions above nor the questions you are entertaining will be answered by your beginning course. They cannot be answered because nobody has the answers *in a form which would satisfy the rigorous criteria of acceptable scientific explanation.* That is, nobody who claims to have the answers can satisfy the demand of the scientist who says, "Show me the evidence."

To be sure, many questions will be posed in your course, and many will be answered. But they will be less grand, less meaningful, less important than you may wish.

Many of us who have chosen the science of behavior as our life's work began our study in psychology with similar or the same unanswerable questions. These questions provided motivation for study, and sooner or later in our development as psychologists we picked one out to focus upon, to try to answer. But once we began to attack our question we immediately faced a number of problems common to all researchers, problems forcing the investigator to recast his question in terms which allow him some hope of finding an answer. One of these problems is that of definition. The scientist must define his terms so that the definition is narrow enough to include just what he wants it to include, and nothing else—clear enough so that other people know what it means, and yet broad enough to be sufficiently important to warrant investigation.

Attempts to construct such definitions almost always involve cutting the original question down to manageable proportions, or, more frequently, cutting it up into several smaller questions, or, more frequently still, discovering that several other preliminary questions must be answered first. It is not at all uncommon to see an investigator shift his focus of interest and become permanently involved in trying to answer one of the narrower or preliminary questions.

The problem of definition is no mean one, as every reader who has ever been involved in an argument with a clever adversary knows. It is often used as a last-ditch defense by someone who does not wish to concede a point. It is used also as a way out by someone who does not wish to expend the effort involved in thinking or working, as when a person argues that there is no point in studying juvenile delinquency because no one even agrees on what juvenile delinquency is! However, the problem of definition is often crucial for answering meaningful questions. With respect to the quest for a scientific understanding of behavior, the definition of terms is a crucial step. Lest the reader get from this discussion the false impression that psychological problems are merely matters of definition, the authors would like to state most emphatically that psychologists do in fact grapple with problems of definition all the time, and that we define our terms with exquisite care. However, let us state equally emphatically that definition is only the first step, albeit a necessary one, toward answering a research question.

To illustrate the above, but primarily to communicate to the reader a feel for why psychologists do the kinds of things they do, let us select one of the students' questions presented at the beginning of this section and try to "answer" it.

ASKING ANSWERABLE QUESTIONS

Why does one's personality change under stress? Clearly, this is an important question, having implications for the behavior of people in riot-torn streets, men at war, men behind the wheel of a car on a busy highway, children being scolded by their parents, students taking exams, women in labor—in short, for the behavior of people under the virtually limitless number of conditions called stressful.

But the question as posed is not amenable to scientific investigation.

Before it can be considered a scientifically meaningful question it must be recast in such a fashion that a scientist can make the *observations* necessary to answer it. These observations must be of situations which are relevant to the question, that is, stressful, and of behaviors which denote, or define, personality change. The observations must be of stimulus situations, environmental conditions, or whatever you may wish to call them, which people would agree are within the meaning of stress. Some particular aspects of the subject's behavior, some set of observable responses, must also be selected for observation to provide a basis for deciding whether or not anything like personality change does, in fact, occur. These observations—of stimuli and responses—must be made under the most rigorously *controlled* conditions possible, and must be *repeatable* by independent investigators. The word *controlled* is a key word in any scientific context. Basically it means that when an investigator wants to observe the effect of some environmental condition on behavior, he must guard religiously against the possibility that it is some other condition which is actually affecting the behavior.

The above paragraph is rather short. It uses simple words. But it epitomizes the essence of science, as science is currently conceived. When someone claims to have the answer to any important question about behavior, he should, as suggested above, also be able to answer the question: Where is the evidence? If he cannot produce the evidence in the form of repeatable, carefully controlled observations of the behavior in question, he has an answer, but his answer cannot be considered in any sense a scientific answer. It may be a poetical or philosophical answer. It may or may not be a very good answer—but whatever it may be, it is not a *scientific* answer.

Let us briefly summarize what has just been stated, and then begin to look carefully at what is involved when a scientist goes about answering questions about the effect of stress on personality.

In order for a question to be answered scientifically, it must be asked so that repeatable, controlled observations of all significant items in the question can be made.

The above is absolutely crucial to your understanding of the science of psychology—and of any science. It is the rock on which the "big" questions founder, and also the rock on which contemporary science is built. A close analysis of our student's question about stress will make that crucial statement more meaningful, and will also help us make the question more meaningful. Let us look at the key words of the question, one by one, in an effort to make clear why the question as posed is unanswerable. By exploring the implications of each term in that question, we will attempt to make it clear why it is absolutely necessary to reduce that big question to a multitude of smaller, perhaps less interesting but at least answerable, ones.

WHY. The reader may have already considered that the very first word in the question is inappropriate. Scientists are basically curious people. They ask about the "why" of things all the time. But when they set about asking answerable questions, the "why" is dropped. Actually if the "why" refers to a question about ultimate causality, then it would be totally inappropriate, since such questions are in the realm of philosophy or religion. If, on the other hand, the "why" is just shorthand for, What is the relationship between . . . or, Under what conditions . . . , then the question could be a strictly legitimate, scientific question, provided the other terms meet the test of observability.

PERSONALITY. Personality is not purple! Nor is it red, yellow, blue, or pink, square, sweet, loud, or hard. *It is not an it.* Personality is an idea that caught on some time in the history of our language. No one ever saw it, smelled it, tasted it, heard it, or touched it. If someone tries to sell you some at $1.98 per pound, he ought to be locked up. If you buy some, you ought to be! It is not an it—it is an idea that caught on. It caught on because the idea of personality has helped men make sense out of their own behavior and the behavior of people around them. In some respects the concept of personality is like the concept of force in physics or valence in chemistry. In the technical terminology of the philosophy of science these ideas, by definition unobservable, are called *hypothetical constructs.* These constructs—like force, valence, gravity, personality—help us make sense out of our world. They help us understand the myriads of events constantly occurring about us. These constructs enable us to bring some order and simplicity to the fantastic complexity the environment constantly presents to our millions upon millions of sense receptors.

Personality is a concept which expresses consistency in behavior. It also expresses inconsistency in a person's behavior as well as differences in behavior between individuals. These are the facts of behavior to which the term applies. For example, when we refer to a particular person as a "basically honest" individual, we are referring to an aspect of personality which cuts across a variety of different situations, and we are also implying a difference between that person and other people—people whom we would not characterize as "basically honest." People frequently refer to a personality characteristic such as honesty as though it were something *inside* the individual, which explains, or makes some sense out of, much of the person's *outside* or observable behavior. In other words, a variety of external, observable behaviors are labeled with a concept which has reference to some postulated, internal, unobservable process. Thus the behavior seems somehow less complex, less mysterious, that is, more understandable. It is important to note that personality is one of these unobservable, hypothetical constructs. It is a useful term in our everyday vocabulary. If it is an idea that has caught on, it has caught on because it is useful—it is a helpful summary description of a class of complex behavior. We can use the term meaningfully in our everyday vocabulary because everyone roughly knows what it describes. In order to gain a scientific understanding of the term over and above our everyday understanding, we must specify clearly those observable behaviors which the concept is generally considered to summarize, those behaviors to which the concept, or construct, is generally considered to refer. Not all of our everyday concepts turn out to be scientifically useful—consider the concepts of luck or women's intuition. The reasoning may seem tortured, but it is not. The word *personality* was "created" sometime long ago to help make sense out of events people saw—out of *observables*. The everyday use of the word indicates that people roughly—even if only very roughly—agree on the referents of the word. If we believe that the term may be scientifically useful as well, and if we elect to use it in a scientific context, we must employ the observables, or some of them, to which personality refers.

Therefore, we must set about looking at those *behaviors* generally considered to be represented by the construct, or idea, of personality; that is, behaviors which differentiate people from one another and behaviors which can be considered characteristic of given individuals. In other words we must now define personality in terms of observable behavior so that we can make the question a scientifically answerable one. However, as was implied above, the idea of personality represents a host of behaviors, and no researcher could possibly investigate all of these various meanings of personality. Therefore, what is done is to select one, two, or perhaps three of these indices of personality for the purpose of making scientific investigation possible. In other words, the question is cut down to manageable proportions.

Let's bring to a more concrete level what is being said.

A partial list of the observable measures of behavior with which different investigators have defined personality or some aspect of personality should illustrate the point.

Responses to inkblot tests
Responses to a test of anxiety
Breathing rate
Heart rate
How many electric shocks one person will deliver to another
What intensity of electric shock one person will deliver to another
How much shock a person can himself tolerate
Pupillary dilation
Sweating
Punching a stand-up rubber clown
Memory tasks
Content of stories to ambiguous pictures
Solution of anagrams
Performance on a verbal learning task
Time it takes a person to free-associate
Attitudes expressed toward strangers on a test
Color preference
Social class
Job preferences
Judgments of facial expressions of others
Judgments of others' speech
Quality of speech
Susceptibility to group pressure
Rapidity of eyeblink conditioning
Content of dreams
Frequency of dreams
Estimation of size of "threatening" objects
Perceptual distortion
Ratings of personality by peers
Ratings of personality by parents
Self-ratings of personality
Judgments by psychiatrists or psychotherapists
Activity of children at play
Analysis of paintings
Hypnotizability

One or more of the above definitions would be selected by a particular investigator as his measure of personality. The choice would depend upon his own specific interests and would be made with great care to suit the purposes of a given investigation. Whatever specific index is selected, two closely related points should be kept in mind:

    1. The original richness and grandeur of the term

personality are lost—sacrificed—to the inviolable rule of rigorous, carefully controlled, repeatable observation. No longer are we talking about personality with all of the lush associations which have been tied to it through use in novels, Hollywood press-agentry, theories such as psychoanalysis, and everyday speech.

2. The questions themselves have changed profoundly. They are no longer dealing with the complex, global concept, personality, but *one measure* of *one aspect* of personality.

CHANGE. Again, everyone knows what the word *change* means. But remember that in a scientific context each word in a research question must be defined not only so that observations can be made, but also so that these observations can be *repeated* by other investigators. In order to do research concerning personality, the construct must be defined in terms of observables. When we talk about observed changes in personality, these changes must be specified in such a fashion that someone else can observe the same changes. Most psychologists strive to specify their concepts quantitatively. One of the most important reasons for doing so is that only after we have assigned numbers to a particular aspect of behavior is it possible to address the question of how much or how many. Only by answering how much or how many can we communicate what we mean by change. Consider the difference between, "the subject's personality changed" and "the subject's heart rate increased from seventy to ninety beats per minute." The first report is couched in nonquantitative terminology, the second in quantitative units of behavior.

The goal of quantification is not always so easily achieved as implied by the example of counting heartbeats. The problems involved in assigning numbers usefully to situations and to behaviors are often subtle and complex. Difficulties of quantification are so omnipresent in psychological research that the set of difficulties is typically referred to with considerable respect as the *problem of measurement*. A discussion of measurement, which, again, is the assignment of numerals to observables (or some characteristics of observables), could have been raised in several places above. Certainly it is relevant to the problem of definition. It could easily have been raised in connection with the extraordinary difficulties involved with the quantification of personality characteristics. It is probably easier for the student, however, to think about the necessity of quantification in terms of the description, or specification, of change. Change can be described verbally, but it is far more convenient and, believe it or not, far *simpler* and more meaningful to describe change quantitatively.

For example, we might say: This medication has reduced the student's anxiety and he now does better on examinations. This verbal description does not specify exactly what was done to induce change. Nor does it clearly state just what changes have occurred. However, the quantification of this statement does clarify the issues. For example, we might rephrase the outcome as follows: After six weeks of taking a certain dosage of a tranquilizer three times a day, the stress of examinations has been reduced to the extent that the student's grade point average has improved 1.5 points. Change can be conceptualized in terms of change in kind and in terms of change in amount. In both cases, numbers can be assigned to specify more clearly the changes observed.

STRESS. Stress is not purple either. It, too, is by definition a nonobservable, hypothetical construct. It, too, has many meanings, summarizing a host of different situations, as well as reactions to these situations, loosely tied together in our everyday speech by a common thread. The various everyday usages of the term *stress* involve a disrupted state of the organism, which could be considered a personality change for the worse. If stress is defined as a disrupted state of the organism and stressors are defined as environmental conditions which cause stress, then the question, Why does one's personality change when under stress? is patently circular. Once we have recast the original question into a question or questions about specific antecedent conditions and their consequences, however, the circularity evaporates. Once the "big" question is properly recast, the scientist can begin looking for the relationships between specific stressors and specific behavioral indices of personality.

The reader may have noted that the authors have again shifted some terminology without warning. We have shifted from talking about the relationship between stress and personality to the relationship between *stressors* (or stimuli which cause stress) and specific behavioral indices of personality. The list of potential stressors is virtually endless, but the following examples should give the reader a fair notion of the range of situations which could be called stressors.

A long, loud noise
An unhappy marriage
Combat
An examination
Unavoidable electric shock
Threat of physical harm
Physical harm
Angry parents

Prolonged deprivation of bodily needs
Bodily illness
Solitary confinement
A long highway trip
A crying child
Personal inadequacies
The memory of a guilt-provoking act
Having one's hand plunged in icewater
Motion pictures of automobile accidents
Motion pictures of operations
Fear of failure
Failure
Extreme heat
Extreme cold
Anticipation of psychological harm
Attacks on one's self-esteem
Insults
An interview by a psychiatrist
A telegram from the government
Being required to solve arithmetic problems rapidly
Combat training
Parachute jumps
Prolonged submersion in a submarine
Waiting for a dentist
Lying on a cart being wheeled to an operating room
Strong, unpleasant odors
Very bright lights
Films of primitive sexual rites
Threat to social status
Snakes
Having rubber snakes dangled in front of you

We have been discussing hypothetical constructs in a fashion which some psychologists and philosophers of science would consider quite appropriate, but which others would regard as loose. In the analysis presented above, a construct might be defined primarily in terms of a set of behavioral indices. For example, the construct of intelligence would be defined in terms of test scores, school performance, success in various occupations, and so forth. Personality, too, is such a construct. On the other hand, there are constructs which are defined in terms of both environmental and behavioral indices. Constructs such as stress, anxiety, frustration, and hunger drive are of this latter sort, being defined by both antecedent conditions and consequent behaviors.

Some psychologists feel that only the concepts which are defined on both the antecedent and consequent sides attain the status of a hypothetical construct, and that these will ultimately prove most theoretically fruitful. For our purposes, and in consideration of the present state of psychological knowledge, we feel it is more useful to adopt the less strict definition.

PUTTING THE PIECES TOGETHER. Now that we have broken the important question about stress into fragments, what is the next step? Or putting the same question into a more formal context, once a research psychologist has analyzed his interests in a fashion similar to that which you have just read, what does he *do?*

Anyone wishing to know anything about the relationship between stress and personality change must select specific stressors to measure or to present to subjects in a systematic fashion, and specific indices of personality to observe and measure. The decisions as to which manipulations and measurements the investigator will select as his definitions of stress and personality are determined by many considerations. One of the primary determinants of these decisions, one which no one talking or writing about psychological research should ever fail to mention, is the individual interests of the person doing the research! Let no mistake be made about the motives of the scientist doing research. While there is no question that work, and even boredom, is involved in many aspects of doing research, the scientist does it because in many ways he finds research exciting and rewarding. For him there is not only the peculiar fascination of working on difficult problems and the enormous satisfaction of solving them, but also the exhilaration of discovery.

It would be nice if we could conclude this section with a set of rules for asking good, answerable questions. It would be nice if we could tell the reader how to ask that set of answerable questions which would most quickly and economically lead to an understanding of the overall relationship between stress and personality. But we cannot. Nobody can. However, we state it as an act of scientific faith that asking and answering one answerable question takes us further along the road to that understanding than asking all of the interesting, important, *un*answerable questions that a whole university full of inquisitive students could ask!

Let us look now at some of the research questions that have been asked, and at least partially answered, about the relationship between stress and personality.

Part II

Some Answers

CHILDHOOD STRESS AND ADULT PERSONALITY

For many years psychologists have been interested in the "grand question": What is the relationship between a person's experiences during childhood and his adult personality? Clearly, this is an extremely broad question, so broad that it is impossible to provide any sort of meaningful answer. In other words, the scientist must break this question down to manageable proportions before considering how to answer it. While one could begin by asking what is meant by *childhood* (that is, what age) and what is meant by *adult personality*, let us first ask: What experiences are we talking about? and What aspects of childhood are we interested in?

Many years ago Sigmund Freud, a Viennese psychiatrist, formulated a theory of behavior centering about the importance of what he called childhood *trauma* or *stress*. His basic notion was that adult personality is profoundly affected by the traumatic or stressful experiences of childhood. Freud argued that as the young child develops he passes through a fixed, universally occurring series of phases, which Freud called the stages of psychosexual development. The first stage was the oral stage during which the infant is almost totally involved with activity concerning the mouth: sucking, eating, lip smacking, gurgling, and so forth. The second stage Freud termed the anal stage. In this stage, he argued, the infant is primarily concerned with activity centering around the anus; elimination, toilet training, smearing feces, and so forth. Freud's third phase, the phallic stage, supposedly finds the child interested in the manipulation of, and activities concerned with, the genitals. In the fourth, or latency, stage the child theoretically drops his interest in bodily zones and becomes involved with school, peers, and becoming socialized. Ideally, after the several stages of development are passed through, the individual has developed into a mature, stable adult. This assumes, according to Freud, that all has gone well during the various periods of development. However, if trauma or stress interferes with the normal developmental process, then personality is affected and the effects are carried into adulthood. Furthermore, Freud argued that the nature of the effects on personality will vary with the stage of development in which the stress occurs, and also with the nature of the stress.

Now how does this brief theoretical outline fit into our scheme of things? We began with the grand and unanswerable question: How does childhood affect adult personality? We have, by introducing some theoretical notions, fit the question into a theoretical context from which specific predictions can be made. We can now ask a question related to some specific aspect of childhood. For example: What will happen to adult personality as a function of stress related to oral activity? This is also an unanswerable question. Again the definition of adult personality is lacking. Also we have not yet defined what is meant by trauma or stress, nor have we defined specifically what is meant by oral activity. What we have done is narrow our grand question to a more specific realm of childhood experience based upon some theoretical notions, and we have also, in general, defined the nature of the experience we want to study (that is, stress or trauma). So let's pursue this narrowing process even further. The major oral activity is eating. We can define another term in our question: What is the effect of stress or trauma related to childhood eating experience on adult personality? Again, the nature of the trauma or stress is undefined, as is adult personality. But the question has been narrowed. Let us now attack the remaining ambiguities.

Clinicians and anthropologists have made observations over the years which have led them to believe that adults who have experienced feeding frustration as infants are competitive and quarrelsome, and tend to hoard food. On the other hand, casual observations have suggested that when children are fed in loving ways and not frustrated they become generous and cooperative adults. So as a result we can again narrow our question, making it less and less grand. We have begun to define what we mean by trauma or stress and we have also begun to delineate what we mean by adult personality. We can now begin to formulate a very crude and preliminary hypothesis: Stress in the form of feeding frustration during infancy will cause the adult to develop personality traits like competitiveness, hoarding, and uncooperativeness.

But how do we go about testing this notion in keeping with the scientific principles outlined previously? First of all, we must ask the very general question: What is the nature of the experimental design needed to test the hypothesis? We could observe two groups of infants, one group whose feeding is accompanied by some relatively severe, frustrating experience, and another group whose feeding is accomplished with "tender, loving care." Of course, we would then have to wait around for twenty or more years, and then make the observations necessary to determine whether or not the predicted differences would appear in the adult personality patterns of the two groups. If they were to appear, and if we had been able to rule out other possible explanations, then we would have confirmed our hypothesis. We would have also lent some support to the theory from which it had been deduced. However, that last "if" is a big one.

It is practically impossible to make all of the observations necessary to preclude the possibility that some other factor besides the frustration caused the difference. Along how many other dimensions do real-life mothers who feed their infants lovingly differ from those who feed them stressfully? Does the answer to that dilemma lie in establishing sufficient control over two groups of infants such that we could guarantee that their childhood experiences were highly similar except that we would feed one group lovingly and the other one stressfully? The answer to the latter question is, of course, a resounding *No*. It would be profoundly unethical for anyone to deal with human beings in such a fashion.

So the obvious experimental design to answer the question of interest is impractical because of the number of years involved. Adding the necessary controls would be unethical, even if possible. So what is the alternative? We could, of course, abandon the question. Or we could use infrahuman organisms, for example, rats. The use of animals is clearly not optimal in terms of our original question because rats are obviously not humans. Nevertheless, with animals we could do the research and we would not have to be concerned with the insoluble ethical and methodological problems which would be involved if we studied children.

Assuming that we decide to approach our question using rats as subjects, we must define the terms in our question so that the relevant manipulations and observations can be made. We must select operations defining the stress of feeding frustration, operations which can be made reliably on rats. We must select indices of personality which can be observed reliably in rats. Perhaps the best way to demonstrate how this is done is to select from the literature an actual experiment dealing directly with the question at hand.

In 1941 a psychologist, J. McV. Hunt, began asking "grand" questions about childhood experiences and adult personality in much the same way as we began this section. He, too, came to the same conclusions regarding the need for using rats. Let us see how he went about defining the terms in the question and how he went about testing the hypothesis.

As we indicated above, one of the first things that had to be decided was: What is meant by *infancy?* On the basis of the rate of biological development of the species, and in light of his question, Hunt decided to focus on a period of time closely following weaning, which in rats occurs approximately twenty-one days after birth. Next, it was necessary to define what is meant by stress or feeding frustration. In the case of his experiment he allowed twenty-four-day-old animals to eat for only ten minutes at a time after being forced to go hungry over varying lengths of time. This treatment lasted for fifteen days. Thus, two of the crucial elements have been defined: childhood and feeding stress or frustration. The next thing to be decided was: What will be called *adulthood?* Again, on the basis of developmental considerations Hunt chose an age of approximately six months to represent the adult rat. Thus at the end of the six-month period he was ready to ask the question: What effect, if any, has the childhood experience of feeding frustration had upon the adult personality? Still another problem of definition had to be resolved. Recall that earlier we referred to some anecdotal and clinical evidence suggesting that feeding stress made people uncooperative, selfish, and so forth. Hunt had to reduce these statements to some aspect of rat behavior which he could measure. He decided to define the aspect of adult personality he would measure as *hoarding behavior,* the amount of food a nonhungry animal would carry back to its cage. This was further specified as the number of food pellets stored over a series of four trials lasting thirty minutes each, one trial per day for four days.

Before continuing with our research example, let us summarize what has been said up to now. We started out with the grand question: What is the effect of childhood experience upon adult personality? Freud's theory, plus some unsystematic observations, helped us narrow the question to: What is the result of feeding frustration on adult personality? As we progressed it became important, for many reasons, to finally reduce our grand question until it now can be stated as: What effect does depriving twenty-four-day-old rats of food over a fifteen-day period have on the storage of food pellets during a series of thirty-minute periods after the rats have matured to six months of age? The question is further specified in that the mature rats were frustrated prior to the hoarding tests by keeping them on a "subsistence diet" for five days. The question is not so grand anymore—but now we can answer it. Let's continue.

There is one very important aspect of scientific research that up to this point has not been included in our discussion of Hunt's research; that is the concept of control. Now that the question has been reduced to manageable size we must include in our experiment the controls necessary to allow us to provide a scientifically meaningful answer.

Since Hunt intended to demonstrate that the stressful childhood experience, as he defined it, had an effect on adult personality, again as he defined it, he had to show that rats which had not received the childhood eating stress did not develop the hoarding behavior. Thus the question becomes one of comparing groups of rats, a frustrated group and a non-frustrated group. In order to make the results of the comparisons more interpretable, Hunt did not just use any two groups of rats. He obtained genetically matched groups of rats by splitting litters in such a fashion that each rat in the experimental group had a genetically similar littermate in the control group.

But Hunt wished to go further. He also wanted to determine if the *particular age during infancy* at which feeding frustration occurred was an important determinant of adult hoarding behavior. In order to answer this aspect of the question, two more groups of rats were needed. One additional group had to undergo the feeding frustration *later* than twenty-four days in infancy. Hunt decided to use thirty-two-day-old rats. A second control group of matched thirty-two-day-old rats had to be given the normal eating exposure. We might diagram the experimental design as follows:

Group	Type of infantile feeding experience	Measure of behavior in adulthood following five days of "subsistence" eating
Experimental I	Frustrated at 24 days of age	Number of pellets hoarded
Control I	Unlimited food	Number of pellets hoarded
Experimental II	Frustrated at 32 days of age	Number of pellets hoarded
Control II	Unlimited food	Number of pellets hoarded

Prior to initiating the hoarding test in adulthood, Hunt observed the rats' behavior while they were sated on food. No differences in hoarding appeared between the groups.

Now there are two major comparisons to make in attempting to answer the question. The first is a comparison between the twenty-four-day-old frustration group and their control group, control I. If, at the end of the six months, experimental group I hoards more pellets than control group I, then Hunt could say that feeding frustration does affect later behavior. If, in addition, experimental group II does not hoard more than control group II, then Hunt would have evidence not only that infantile feeding-frustration affects later behavior, but that the time of such infantile frustration is crucial. If experimental group II does hoard more than their controls, this would provide further evidence that infantile frustration is important, but would not support the contention that the specific time of such frustration is of any consequence. If the hoarding was found in the twenty-four-day-old frustration group and not in the thirty-two-day-old frustration group then Hunt could argue that not only is it feeding frustration in infancy but feeding frustration early in infancy that is important in determining adult hoarding behavior.

So the experiment demands four groups of rats—all necessary to answer our not very grand, but answerable, question. What did Hunt find and how do his answers relate to the grand question?

First of all, the twenty-four-day-old frustration group hoarded more in later life than did control group I. Experimental group II did not differ in hoarding behavior from control group II. In fact, the latter three groups did not differ from one another with respect to hoarding, but they all hoarded less than the twenty-four-day-old group.

Can we now say that childhood feeding frustration leads to adult hoarding behavior? No. What we can say is that, given the specific operations used in Hunt's experiment, feeding frustration induced in rats at twenty-four days of age produced hoarding at six months of age while the same frustration in thirty-two-day-old rats did not effectively produce adult hoarding. Can we say anything about human behavior? Not directly. We can't even say much about childhood or adulthood, since it is very difficult to talk in these terms when we are dealing with rats. But there is one point that we cannot forget. While the grand question has not been answered we have more information related to it than we had before. We now know that certain kinds of stress will affect certain kinds of later behavior at least in one species. The findings are highly consistent with certain theories regarding the effects of early experience on later behavior. They *lend support* to the theories with which they are consistent, and this is important. Continued research with a variety of manipulations of stress and a variety of measures of personality in a variety of species will perhaps lead us closer to an understanding of the relationships involved. Perhaps an understanding of the laws relating early stress experience to adult behavior in infrahuman species will enable us to look at human behavior in a new light and to understand it more thoroughly. In other words, perhaps seeing the relevant factors in the relatively controllable experiments with infrahuman organisms will tell us what to look for in the less controllable studies of human behavior.

One final comment on the Hunt study should be made. While the hypothesis was confirmed and the theory from which it was deduced was thereby supported, the theory was in no sense *proven*. There are any number of theoretical positions besides Freudian psychoanalysis which postulate long-term effects of disadvantageous early experience. In addition to the alternative-theory problem, Hunt's study is but one study—with one manipulation of stress and one measure of personality in one species. While the feeding-frustration question has been partially answered, it is only one small segment of the psychoanalytic theory of personality. A thorough, scientific test of the entire body of Freudian theory is actually inconceivable. If the big questions are untestable, then so are the grand theories.

ONE EFFECT OF STRESS ON THE BODY

The term *executive* calls up many images: big office, big desk, big car, and big man handling big problems. In a psychology-conscious America it also calls up the image of that big man as a distressed, driven man, ulcer-ridden by the recurrent pressure to make decisions affecting not only his own life but the lives of many other people. To the extent that this image mirrors reality, it reflects an insight into a relationship between stress and one of the most fundamental forms of behavior—and one of the most fundamental characteristics of personality—*emotional* behavior. Our everyday language vividly depicts the emotional reactions of a man under stress with such phrases as, "He's eating his insides out," or "Something is gnawing at him." It seems, in short, that it is commonplace today (though it certainly was not in the past) to recognize that psychological stress can have far-reaching effects not only behaviorally, but physiologically as well. But just how well understood is the relationship between stress and personality —between stress and the behaviors which produce physiological damage such as ulcers?

There have been some fascinating scientific attempts to uncover the key elements in the development of ulcer-producing emotional behavior under conditions of stress. One of the most fascinating of these attempts is the research program carried on by Joseph V. Brady and others at the Walter Reed Army Institute of Research (Brady, 1958).

Brady and his colleagues began this program with a somewhat different focus of interest. They had spent several years on the more general problem of the relation between stress and emotionality before some unexpected results induced them to concentrate on the relation between stress and ulceration. In their emotionality research they had settled on monkeys as subjects. If the use of infrahuman subjects needs any further justification, let us quote Brady. "Animals obviously cannot provide wholly satisfactory experimental models of human mind-body interactions. They can, however, be studied under controlled conditions, and it is through animal experiments that we are finding leads to the cause of ulcers as well as to the effect of emotional stress on the organism in general" (Brady, 1958, p. 96). An experimenter cannot, of course, manipulate stress. He can, however, manipulate certain aspects of the subject's environment in such a fashion that observers would generally agree is stressful. The kind of manipulation that Brady and his colleagues used was the placement of an animal into a restraining chair and then conditioning the subject. By condition in this study we mean having the animal learn to press a lever regularly to avoid electric shocks. The restraining chair served the function of making sure the subject was where the experimenter wanted him when he wanted him. The monkey could not run away and escape the electric shock, for example. Thus, in more general terms, the restraining chair was serving as a control factor, eliminating extraneous stimuli which might influence the emotional responses of the animal from entering into the experiment. This is extremely important, since the experimenters were interested in observing the effects of their conditioning procedures on emotional responses. This particular control introduced by the experimenters, however, in and of itself seemed to be introducing unwanted influences into the research. The physical restraint imposed upon these energetic monkeys was of such a nature that the restraint itself elicited emotional responses. The team of investigators decided to take some physiological measures to get some information about the internal biological effects of the chair and conditioning procedures. A small preliminary study showed that the stress situation did, in fact, radically change the level of certain hormones in the animals' blood. This finding encouraged the researchers to do a large-scale study with nineteen monkeys. After a relatively short period of time, the unexpected event referred to above brought the research to a halt. Many of the monkeys died! Postmortem examinations revealed that many of the monkeys had developed massive stomach ulcers, which are relatively rare in laboratory monkeys. Now one of the marks of a true scientist is to know when to be surprised. As a very influential American psychologist, B. F. Skinner, has put it, "When you run onto something interesting, drop everything else and study it" (Skinner, 1959, p. 363). Brady and his colleagues knew when to be surprised, and they now shifted the focus of their research program to factors producing ulceration. They were convinced from extensive prior research that it could not be the influence of the chair alone, but they had to design an experiment which would somehow factor out (that is, control) the effect of the restraining chair. The particular conditioning procedure which they had employed provided a good starting point from which to work; it seemed to be the primary source of the fatal stress. However, the conditioning procedure itself is complex and the effect on the animals may be due to any one of several aspects of the situation, or perhaps to the joint effect of several acting simultaneously.

Brady and his colleagues controlled for many of the unwanted sources of potential influences with a very ingenious experimental setup. They continued using the restraining chair for their experimental animals, but each experimental animal was paired with a control animal which was held in a restraining chair in exactly the same way and for exactly the same period of time as the experimental animal. Furthermore, each time the experimental animal failed to press the lever which prevented the shock and got a shock, the *control animal also got a shock*, of precisely the same duration and precisely the same intensity. The control animal also had a lever, identical with that in the experimental animal's chamber, but one which was nonfunctional (that is, it could not prevent shock). Consider for a moment what the experimenters have accomplished with this so-called yoked-chair apparatus. The two monkeys are in virtually identical environments, same restraint, same visual surroundings, same sounds—same everything *except* for the condition which the experimenters suspected was crucial—the psychological stress of having to press the lever.

The details of the experimental procedure are important. The "executive monkey" was required to press the lever at least once every twenty seconds in order to avoid a 5-milliampere, 60-cycle, .5-second electrical shock. The monkey was required to "work" on a six-hour-on, six-hour-off schedule. No shocks at all were delivered during the "off" periods, with these periods being defined for the animals by the presence of a red light.

WHAT HAPPENED? The executive learned his task very well. He averaged between fifteen and twenty lever presses per minute and didn't even slow down. Until he died! After twenty-three days of the conditioning procedure the executive died—without warning—of a massive perforated ulcer. The control monkey, who had been equally restrained and equally shocked was alright. A second pair of animals was subjected to the same conditioning procedure and again the executive monkey died of ulcers—this time after twenty-five days. A third executive lasted but nine days, and a fourth, forty-eight. Autopsies on all four of the executive monkeys revealed massive gastrointestinal damage, while none of the autopsies on the controls revealed any gastrointestinal complications at all. The ulcers were truly psychosomatic—actual physical tissue damage resulting from psychological stress.

The research team continued their experimentation and homed in still further on the nature of the relationships involved. There was some evidence that social factors may be important, since the executive and control could and did communicate with each other. They, therefore, studied several more pairs of monkeys, keeping all the contingencies the same as before, save one. This time they isolated the two members of a pair from one another. It didn't help. The executives developed ulcers and died; the controls did not.

In an effort to vary the level of stress and observe the effects on ulceration, the researchers tried schedules of shock-on and shock-off periods other than six on, six off. They expected that an eighteen on, six off (eighteen hours of decisions and six hours of rest) regime would speed up the ulceration—but it did not. The experimenters were surprised to find that none of these monkeys developed ulcers. They tried thirty minutes on—thirty minutes off, with shocks *every two seconds!* The executives worked at their bar pressing frantically for weeks—but again none of them developed ulcers! No other schedule of work and rest periods (perhaps it would be more appropriate to say stress and rest periods) which they tried led to the development of stomach ulcers.

Clearly the emotional stress, in order to produce ulceration, had to be intermittent, and since not all intermittent schedules "worked," the stress cycles apparently coincided with some natural gastrointestinal cycle of the organism. In order to get a clearer picture of what was happening, the experimenters analyzed the acidity of some of the monkeys' stomachs over the duration of the experiment. Again they came up with some surprising findings. Stomach acidity remained fairly low and constant during stress, but rose sharply during the rest period! The sharpest rise occurred during rest periods following six-hour stress periods, while there was none at all following a one-hour stress session. This surely describes one link of what must be a long chain of events which intervene between psychological stress and the production of ulcers—and *may* be relevant to an understanding of the stressful conditions which lead to ulcers in human executives as well.

Brady and his colleagues have by no means fully described the relationship between stress and ulceration, much less the relationship between stress and personality. Brady himself takes pains to point out that there is a great deal that they do *not* know. For example, what other kinds of stress might have the same effects? What other effects did their procedures generate which they might have failed to measure, simply because they were not looking for them? Is there any other way of detecting ulcers in the monkeys as reliable as a postmortem? There are many such questions, and, if the reader does not mind even more repetition, each of these would have to be broken down into answerable questions!

Brady and his co-workers, unlike Hunt, were not attempting to test an aspect of a comprehensive theory. They were, like Hunt, asking at the outset an important question. And like Hunt, they answered not the big question, but highly specific questions, or, as it may be conceived, particular aspects of an important question.

STRESS AND AFFILIATION

We began our discussion by asking an unanswerable question: What is the effect of stress upon personality? We have seen how two researchers have attempted to answer this question by chopping it up into smaller, more manageable parts. Up to now in our discussion these parts have required the use of animals as experimental subjects. Let us now look at some research that attacks part of the problem, using human subjects—female college students at the University of Minnesota.

Stanley Schachter is a psychologist who has been interested in the question of how and why people relate to one another. More specifically, he has been interested in why some people seem to be driven to be around other people a great deal of the time, while others seem to have less need to be in groups. Thus, in general, Schachter has been interested in the *problem of affiliation*. Let's see how this interest has led him to study the relationship between stress and personality, and how his experimental problem developed (Schachter, 1959).

There has been a great deal of speculation and anecdotal evidence suggesting that social isolation produces anxiety, or, in other words, is stressful. Because of "intuitive reasons," as Schachter put it, it seemed reasonable to expect that stress-producing situations would lead to an increase in "affiliative tendencies." Putting this into our framework, Schachter began to ask the question: How does stress or anxiety affect one aspect of personality, a desire to be with others? Clearly this is an unanswerable question as it is now stated. The operations needed to carry out a scientific study of the question are unspecified. As yet we don't know how anxiety is defined and we are even less clear concerning what is meant by "desire to be with others."

As was true in our previous examples it was necessary to decide how to define stress. Schachter chose to define stress in terms of a situation in which the subjects were led to anticipate painful stimulation. The operations he used were relatively simple. He ushered the girls into a room full of electronic equipment and he had a confederate tell them they were going to participate in an experiment on the effects of electric shock. This confederate also discussed things such as electroshock therapy, electrocution, and so forth. He then told the subjects that they were to receive painful shocks so that the effects could be studied scientifically. The exact instructions were as follows (Schachter, 1959, p. 13):

> Allow me to introduce myself, I am Dr. Gregor Zilstein of the Medical School's Departments of Neurology and Psychiatry. I have asked you all to come today in order to serve as subjects in an experiment concerned with the effects of electrical shock.
>
> (Zilstein paused ominously, then continued with a seven- or eight-minute recital of the importance of research in this area, citing electroshock therapy, the increasing number of accidents due to electricity, and so on. He concluded in this vein:)
>
> What we will ask each of you to do is very simple. We would like to give each of you a series of electric shocks. Now, I feel I must be completely honest with you and tell you exactly what you are in for. These shocks will hurt, they will be painful. As you can guess, if, in research of this sort, we're to learn anything at all that will really help humanity, it is necessary that our shocks be intense. What we will do is put an electrode on your hand, hook you into apparatus such as this (Zilstein points to the electrical-looking gadgetry behind him), give you a series of electric shocks, and take various measures such as your pulse rate, blood pressure, and so on. Again, I do want to be honest with you and tell you that these shocks will be quite painful but, of course, they will do no permanent damage.

Thus the situation was designed to include a specific, repeatable set of operations which most observers would agree would produce stress or anxiety. Now it was necessary to define the aspect of personality to be studied, the desire to be with others, or affiliation. In order to explain how this was defined, we will outline the experiment. Remember the question is: How does stress affect the desire to be with others? What type of experimental design is necessary to answer the question? First of all we need subjects who are anxious or stressed, but how will we be able to evaluate their behavior unless we have some behavior for purposes of comparison? Clearly we also need a group of subjects who are not anxious. Thus we have the beginnings of an experimental design. Anxious versus nonanxious subjects are to be compared in terms of which group indicates more of a desire to be with others. How is this handled in terms of operations? We already have seen how anxiety was produced—how about the low-anxious or nonstressed group? These people were brought into the same room minus the electrical equipment. Essentially they were told that they were to participate in a study of the effects of electric shock but that there would be no pain involved and nothing to fear. This operation defines the low-anxious or nonstressed group. The exact instructions were (Schachter, 1959, p. 13):

> I have asked you all to come today in order to serve as subjects in an experiment concerned with the effects of electric shock. I hasten to add, do not let the word "shock" trouble you; I am sure that you will enjoy the experiment.
>
> (Then precisely the same recital on the importance of the research, concluding with:)
>
> What we will ask each one of you to do is very simple. We would like to give each of you a series of very mild electric shocks. I assure you that what you will feel will not in any way be painful. It will resemble more a tickle or a tingle than anything unpleasant. We will put an electrode on your hand, give you a series of very mild shocks and measure such things as your pulse rate and blood pressure, measures with which I'm sure you are all familiar from visits to your family doctor.

We still need to define affiliation. Let's continue with the experiment and see how this was handled. Once the experimental manipulations were completed all subjects were told that there would be a ten-minute delay while the equipment was set up.

During this period, they were told that they could wait in some other rooms which were very comfortable. The essential part of these instructions, however, entailed telling the subjects that they could either wait alone or wait with other subjects who were also participants in the experiment. They were then given a questionnaire with five choices:

1. *I very much prefer being alone*

2. *I prefer being alone*

3. *I don't care very much*

4. *I prefer being together with others*

5. *I very much prefer being together with others.*

Each subject was asked to indicate a preference and it was the response to this scale that defined affiliation. The subjects were never shocked. Once they answered the questionnaire, the experiment was completed, and Schachter explained the whole procedure to all subjects so that they understood what he had done and why.

Before looking at the findings of the research let us summarize what we have done so far. We began with the grand and unanswerable question: How does stress affect personality? We saw that Schachter was interested in one aspect of personality, affiliation, and that he asked the narrower question: How does stress affect the need to affiliate with others? He then reduced his question so that it became: How does telling people they are going to be painfully shocked affect their response to a series of questions relating to affiliation as compared to the effect of telling people they will be shocked but experience no pain?

What were the results? Schachter used a total of sixty-two subjects, thirty-two in the stress group and thirty in the no-stress group. Twenty stressed subjects elected to "be together," nine indicated they didn't care while only three chose to be alone. Of the no-stress subjects ten wished to be together, eighteen didn't care and two wished to be alone. These findings clearly suggest that anxiety increased the tendency to be with others. But Schachter was not satisfied with this answer. He argued that even though it seems that stress produced the desire to affiliate, the experiment did not tell us *why* people want to affiliate when they are anxious. In fact, he pointed out that there may be a number of reasons for his results. For example, does the choice to be together represent a desire to be with *certain* people, people who are in the same miserable situation? The previous experiment cannot answer this question. It would be important to determine whether stress produces a drive which is very general, that is, produces a broad affiliation need, or if, on the other hand, stress produces a specific need to be with others in the same plight. This latter explanation is a kind of misery-loves-company interpretation.

So the first experiment has suggested a second. The new question is: Given that stress produces a desire to be with others, can these others be just anybody or are they people who are undergoing the same stress? Clearly if Schachter wants to interpret the findings of the first experiment in light of this second question he should use operational definitions similar to those in the first experiment and change only what is necessary to answer the second question. Let's see what he did. First of all the question requires only stressed subjects. We already know from the first experiment that stress produces affiliative tendencies. So Schachter used the exact same instructions in the second experiment. But *all* of the subjects were told that the shock would be painful. There was one difference, however. In the first experiment the subjects were in groups when they got the instructions. In the second experiment they were introduced to the procedure individually. This was necessary so as to make it possible to interpret the results clearly. That is, we wouldn't be able to answer the question without confusion if the subjects knew each other.

Once all the subjects had undergone the instructions it was necessary to do something that would allow Schachter to measure their affiliative preferences. Therefore, he again changed the procedure from the first experiment. As before, all subjects were told that they had to wait for ten minutes. This time, however, some were told they could either wait alone or with other girls who were discussing things with their advisors. The rest of the subjects were told they could wait alone or with other girls taking part in the same experiment as themselves. Again, the measure of affiliation was a questionnaire. The items were changed, however, so that the research question could be answered. The scale for this second experiment included the following six statements and the subjects were asked to check one:

1. *I very much prefer being alone*

2. *I prefer being alone*

3. *I slightly prefer being alone*

4. *I slightly prefer being together with others*

5. *I prefer being together with others*

6. *I very much prefer being together with others*

Again, once the experiment was completed the whole thing was explained to the participants. Now let us see what the results were. There were twenty girls in the experiment. Ten girls were given the choice of being alone or with other girls participating in the experiment. The ten remaining were given the choice of being alone or with girls who were talking to their advisors. The results were very clear. The girls who had the choice of being alone or with others participating in the experiment chose to be with the group significantly more than did those who had the choice of being alone or with those not in the experiment. Thus, Schachter was able to refine further the answer to his initial research question. He could now state: Given the conditions of the previous experiment, anxious people tend to affiliate with others who are in the same "trouble," at least when compared to nonanxious people as presently defined. This sounds like a fine and direct answer, and indeed it is. But this is not the end. There are many other questions still unanswered, even within the framework of this somewhat limited question on stress and affiliation. For example, would the same results occur if male rather than female subjects were used? Is the affiliation-stress relationship discovered here limited to college students—who are for the most part, middle-class, white Protestants? Schachter was able to shed some light on the question of the specificity of affiliation within the context of his experimental conditions. A question that still must be answered is: How specific must the stress stimuli be? That is, will anything that makes people anxious also make them want to seek out the company of others, or must the stress be of a certain type? We could raise many interesting and important questions suggested by this research. But the point is that these two studies have attacked only a very small part of the already fragmented grand question. They are interesting and well-done experiments. They provide a bit of information we did not have before. We know a little more about personality and stress. But as the reader can see from the few questions stated above there is not yet a complete answer to the very general question of how stress and affiliation are related. A more complete answer will come only after much more research, and even then it will not be an answer to the grand question: How does stress affect personality?

STRESS AND LEARNING

We have seen that there are a number of ways that the general question, Why does personality change under stress? can be approached. We should recognize that this question is stated so as to imply that everyone's personality changes under stress and that a stressful situation for one person is necessarily a stress situation for another. As yet, we have not dealt with one fundamental issue which in some ways lies at the heart of our "big question." That is, Why does one person "break" in certain situations while another person does not? Why do some soldiers run from the battlefield while others stay and fight? Why do some people "fall apart" during a crisis while others remain "cool"? Basically we are asking two questions here: (1) Why do people differ in their reactions to stress? and (2) Why are some situations stressors for some people and not for others? One possible but very general answer to both questions is learning. That is, people *learn* either adaptive or maladaptive responses to stress. Also, individuals *learn* to respond to certain stimuli or situations as being stressful and other stimuli or situations as being nonstressful.

From this general point of view one person's experience in a given situation may cause him to respond later to that and similar situations with fear (in other words, the situation has become a stressor), while another person's experience with the same situation may produce no fear responses.

We are dealing here with a fundamental issue in psychology, that of individual differences. While individual differences can arise from biological sources (for example, genetic, constitutional, etc.) psychologists have suggested in many contexts that some significant differences among people are learned differences. Now, how does this apply to our questions regarding stress? We could ask: *How* do people learn to respond to certain situations as stressors? This takes for granted that individual differences in what *constitutes* a stressor *can be learned*. The question of how people learn is a query about the learning process itself. Perhaps a more basic question would be, *Can* people learn to respond to situations or stimuli as stressors? This is a question to which Neal Miller (1948) addressed himself a number of years ago. He was essentially interested in the question of whether learned fears are similar in their effects to the fears of "built-in" stressors, such as electric shock or loud noise. In the terms of our book one could look at Miller's research as asking the question, Can someone learn to react to a certain situation with fear (that is, is the situation stressful) when the same situation previously did *not* elicit fear?

You are already familiar with the notion that some research in psychology must be carried out with animals as subjects, so we will not labor the point here. The study of fear and the acquisition of fear is clearly an area in which many questions are asked which simply cannot be investigated using humans as subjects. Miller's experiment was designed to answer one such question. He chose rats as subjects.

Up to the time of Miller's experiment it was a well-established fact that animals and humans will learn habits, or responses, to escape from stressors such as pain, heat, shock, and so forth. But Miller was able to show that once a situation, which had not been stressful before, is associated with pain an animal will learn a *new* response to escape it. The situation has become a stressor as a function of learning experiences in the same sense that heat or shock is a stressor. Like heat or shock the situation can motivate the learning of new responses. Let us see how Miller demonstrated this. First of all, we have to recognize that the terms of the question as so far stated are much too general. As in all of our other research examples, words like stress, fear, neutral, learned, etc., must be reduced to operations. To see how this was accomplished, perhaps it would be best to begin by describing the apparatus used in the experiment.

A 36 x 6 x 8½-inch box was built and divided into two 18-inch compartments. One of these compartments was painted white and had a floor made of metal rods which could be electrified. The second compartment was painted black and had a solid, nonelectrifiable floor. The two compartments were separated by a door which could be opened by turning a wheel inside the box, by pressing a bar inside the box, or by the experimentor pressing a button.

In this experiment the neutral stimulus was the white compartment *before* the grid floors were electrified. In the present context, neutral means, as we shall see, that subjects showed no preference for either the white or the black compartment prior to experiencing shock. This stimulus was, of course, made up of all of the cues available in the compartment including color, shape, and feel of the bars on the animals' feet. The painful or stressful stimulus was represented by electric shock. Miller hoped to show that rats would learn to fear the white box after being shocked there. But how? There was basically a series of four questions which had to be answered or steps to be accomplished in order to establish this important relationship.

First, it was necessary to show that the white box was, in fact, a neutral stimulus (not yet a stressor). Next it was necessary to associate this neutral stimulus with the stressor (shock) so that animals would have the opportunity to learn to fear the white box and to escape from it. The third step was to find out if the white compartment really had become a stressor (did the learning really occur?). If these three steps could be accomplished one could argue that a neutral or non-stressful situation can, through learning, become a stressor. But Miller did not wish to stop there. He asked a fourth question. As we have said, it was well known that organisms could learn to escape from painful situations. However, a very interesting and important question was, Will a stimulus that has *become* a stressor via learning (in this case the white box) now be capable of motivating escape behavior all by itself? Can such a learned stressor motivate new learning when painful shocks are no longer presented in the situation? In terms of the present experiment, once the white compartment becomes a stressor can it motivate the learning of a *new* escape response? Now how about the operations used in these four stages?

    Miller decided to use twenty-five rats as subjects. His first step, aimed at demonstrating that the white compartment was a nonstressful stimulus, was to put each subject into the box for one minute with the door between compartments open. He then observed the animals' behavior. In no case did the rats show any tendency either to stay in *or* to avoid either of the two compartments. Thus Miller assumed that being in the white compartment was a neutral, or nonstressful, situation for the rat. Clearly, being in the white compartment is no more stressful than being in the black, at least, when stress is measured in terms of preference. If subjects had tended to avoid the white compartment then it would not have been possible to assume neutrality and another operation (or situation) would have been used.

    In order to attach fear to what had now been established as a neutral situation, the experimenter next placed each subject in the white compartment for ten trials with shock-induced pain. Briefly, these trials involved putting the subjects in the compartment, turning on shock (or in later trials putting animals in with shock already on), and opening the door for them with the experimenter's button. All of the animals ran rapidly through the door into the black compartment. Fear or stress is *inferred* from the fact that electric shock produced the response of running from the white compartment to the black compartment. But a crucial question remains: Has the white compartment itself become a stressor? That is, has fear now been associated with a previously neutral stimulus so that rats will now escape from the white compartment when no shock is administered? To answer this question Miller next placed the subjects into the white compartment with *no shock on* and for five trials he observed that *all* animals continued to run rapidly through the opened door. If we compare this behavior to the behavior observed in the apparatus prior to the shock trials, it is clear that the animals' behavior has changed! Where before they had shown *no* tendency to avoid or escape the white compartment, they now escaped rapidly from it even though no shock was present. The white compartment is clearly no longer neutral. In very general terms we can say that the subjects have learned to fear a neutral stimulus. Note, however, that these general terms have, in reality, been reduced considerably to specific operations. Neutrality was defined by operations which demonstrate that the subjects had no preference for one box or the other. Fear was first defined in terms of running from one compartment to the other during shock. Now we are saying that the white compartment itself is a stressor—that is, it causes fear. It is a stressor in that subjects now run from it when no stimuli which are innately painful are present. Fear, again, is inferred from running. We argue that learning has taken place because a change in the behavior of the organism has occurred as a function of experience. A preference for the black box has been established and is defined in terms of the five trials in which all rats ran from the white to the black.

The next question is: Can this new, learned stressor motivate the learning of a different escape response? In other words, can this now nonneutral situation have the same effect as the shock stressor in the sense that the animals will acquire some new response to escape it? Not only is this an interesting question in and of itself, but it is an important question in terms of making sense out of the experiment so far. One could argue that the white compartment really has not become a stressor at all. An argument could be made that the animals escaped in the five nonshock trials because they learned a running habit in response to shock and that this habit simply persisted through the few nonshock trials. This argument would not be meaningful if the subjects were able to learn a totally new response to get away from the white compartment.

Miller now modified the apparatus so that turning the wheel in the white compartment would open the door. Then he put the rats in the white compartment with no shock and with the door closed. Animals were kept there for one hundred seconds unless they turned the wheel and escaped. All subjects received sixteen such trials and the time it took them to open the door was recorded.

Thirteen of the twenty-five animals learned to turn the wheel and escape the white compartment. For eleven of these thirteen, the amount of time that they spent in the compartment on each trial before turning the wheel decreased sharply as trials progressed. In other words, learning was occurring for over one-half of the subjects with the only apparent fear stimuli being the cues from the previously neutral white compartment! This compartment not only had become a stressor but also could function in a way similar to the shock stressor —it could provide the basis for the acquisition of a totally new response. Escape learning is defined here by the fact that subjects opened the door and by the fact that their performance over trials, measured by speed of responding, improved.

But Miller was not through. He asked yet another question: What if wheel turning was no longer an effective response? What if turning the wheel no longer opened the door and led to escape? Would the animals learn yet *another* escape response? To explore this question, the thirteen rats that had learned to wheel-turn were put back into the white compartment. However, this time the wheel would not open the door. The animals had to press a bar (the new response to be learned) to escape into the black side of the box. Within ten trials, all thirteen subjects were pressing the bar to escape. Not only that, twelve of these animals improved over trials; the time it took them to make the response once they were placed in the apparatus got shorter and shorter. Again learning was occurring! Miller points out that at first animals did wheel-turn, but this ineffective response was soon abandoned in favor of bar pressing. So it was demonstrated that the previously neutral compartment had become something more than a momentary stressor. It had become powerful enough to motivate the learning of a wheel-turning response and powerful enough to motivate the abandoning of that response in favor of yet another response, bar pressing.

What has all this told us about our grand question, Why does personality change under stress? How did we get what may seem to be so far afield? Let's review what has happened. We have argued that in order to understand the relationships between stress and personality (assuming we clearly define *these* constructs) it would be important to know why some people behave adaptively in the face of stress while others do not. Also, it would be important to know how some particular situations become stressors for one person and not for another. (Recall the argument that these individual differences may be due to the different learning experience that people have encountered regarding stress.)

Of course this is a very general and, in the scientific sense, unsatisfactory answer. Multitudes of experiments are suggested, however, by the basic proposition. One small but important question raised is: Can a situation become a stressor via a learning experience? If this question can be reduced to operations, and Miller did this, then we have added one bit of information which puts us a little closer to a scientifically meaningful answer to our grand, general question.

Interpreting the Miller experiment broadly, we can say that Miller was able to show, at least within the limits of his experiment, that organisms can *learn to fear* biologically harmless situations. Also, he has shown that having learned to fear, this learning experience can provide the basis for *additional* learning. Furthermore, he has demonstrated that organisms can *change* responses to stress as a function of learning.

All of these broad interpretations or answers appear to be consistent with the data. But we must be careful in generalizing from the findings. Strictly speaking, what Miller's research tells us is: Given certain organisms (rats of a particular age and strain) and certain situations (his experimental apparatus) and certain stressors (shock), particular responses (running escape, wheel turning, bar pressing) can be acquired in a given number of trials. Beyond this, we must use great caution in our interpretations of the data and our extrapolations from the experiment. As with other research, questions like, How general are Miller's findings? must be considered. It would be an error, however, to take the findings too lightly. The results are important. From the standpoint of understanding complex human responses to stress, a small, but well-defined, bit of evidence has been obtained which moves us closer to answers related to the "grand question."

If you recall, we said in the very beginning of this book that the study of human behavior is so complex, and the amount of data gathered and yet to be gathered so voluminous, that "in actual practice the psychologist studies intensively some small aspect of one of the so-called simpler phenomena . . . to understand some small piece of the environment-organism interaction."

THE EFFECT OF PROFOUND ISOLATION ON PERSONALITY

The original question of why personality changes under stress has been explored from several different vantage points. In this section we would like to look at a definition of the term *stress* and its effects on personality that is radically different from the preceding meanings, and one which reflects a problem of considerable social significance.

What are the effects on personality of an environment which is so bare that the person is left with essentially nothing to see, hear, feel, smell or taste—and nothing to do? In a word, what are the effects of *sensory deprivation?*

Perhaps you have never thought about it in these

terms, but if a person is to function in a reasonably normal fashion, it helps a great deal to have an environment which provides at least some minimal level of stimulation. The expression, "it helps a great deal" may be an understatement; we shall see. You may have found yourself at one time or another in a situation which was so unspeakably boring that you noticed sharp differences in yourself. You may have been much more irritable than under ordinary circumstances, or you may have found yourself talking or singing to yourself, or looking about for things to do which you would not even consider doing under more normal circumstances. An example of this would be watching a terrible TV program, one which you would never watch normally, just because there's nothing else to do. Perhaps you have tried to solve some sort of problem while you were having difficulty going to sleep. If so, you probably had trouble arriving at a solution as you lay quietly in a dark, silent room. It seems difficult to function in an environment which provides an extremely low level of stimulation. There are, of course, instances of relatively complete and prolonged deprivation. You may have read about some of the strange effects on people of the awesome monotony encountered during exploration of the polar icecaps. Or you may have read about the problems encountered on long solitary sea voyages that some men undertake voluntarily, and that others are forced to endure because of shipwreck. Another severe deprivation condition is, of course, solitary confinement in prison. While there may be high levels of light energy or sound energy present in these situations, there is virtually no change in the input, *no environmental variability,* which is the essence of stimulation. The psychological effects of such prolonged social isolation, prolonged lack of environmental variation, and prolonged physical privations are extraordinary. Some men have come out of deprivation experiences like the ones cited above with serious emotional disturbances. Almost all have reported having experienced serious disturbances of psychological functions while under such deprivation conditions. Commonly reported have been hallucinations (seeing, hearing, or feeling "things" that are not there), delusions (false beliefs, such as the belief that one has just communicated with the dead, or that one has just discovered the key to the great mysteries of the universe), inability to perform routine tasks, inability to concentrate, and so forth.

Perhaps you have also read or seen movies about a phenomenon with the somewhat sinister name of *brainwashing.* Brainwashing may seem unrelated to the above, but it will become clear that it is intimately related. In fact, sensory deprivation seems to be one very important ingredient of brainwashing.

Many people were surprised and disturbed at reports coming out of Russia in the 1950's concerning trials of some purged, major political figures. The Russians were getting obviously false, even fantastic, confessions from these people, and getting them in public trials! What was perhaps most surprising was the behavior of the defendants. Formerly fiery Communists were now docile, passive men. Men who had been bears had become lambs. What new, powerful means of producing personality changes did the Russians have? Also, reports of even more far-reaching programs of thought reform were coming out of Red China, but these received relatively little publicity. The events which really upset the American public, however, were the accounts of the seemingly absolute control which the Red Chinese and North Koreans were able to achieve over American prisoners of war. It was at this time that the word *brainwashing* became part of the English language. The Red Chinese were effecting radical revisions in personality. How they were doing it was not understood. Many of the UN soldiers were totally unprepared to cope with the methods, whatever they were.

And here begins the scientific tale. In the early 1950's, D. O. Hebb of McGill University was requested by the Canadian government to investigate the so-called brainwashing phenomenon. Hebb theorized that the extraordinary alterations in behavior in brainwashing were perhaps the results of an extraordinarily monotonous environment. This seemed at least possible, considering that changes in the beliefs, perceptions, and feelings of many individuals had been temporarily brought about by the natural deprivation conditions previously mentioned. Hebb did not "just happen" to be the scientist who saw the relationship. He had just published a major theoretical book, *The Organization of Behavior* (1949). In this book he placed a very great emphasis on the importance of a continuing level of sensory stimulation for normal psychological functioning. He had concluded that some minimal level of sensory input was absolutely necessary for the maintenance of normal thought, feeling, emotion, etc. Therefore, he argued, severe restriction of sensory input would have serious consequences for the organism, and perhaps this was the key to the profound personality alterations found in brainwashing.

Hebb decided that a proper understanding of these seemingly diverse influences on the person could best be attained by the experimental approach. That is, he decided to manipulate the environment systematically in order to create deprivation. There are important reasons for studying the question experimentally. If you compare a deprivation environment with a normally stimulating environment, the two differ in many ways. Unless the environment is brought under the control of the experimenter, it is impossible to tell which difference or combination of differences produces the behavioral change.

In the deprivation situations there is not only the prolonged lack of environmental variability but there are also factors such as prolonged social isolation, frequently prolonged restriction of activity, disruption of sleep cycles, etc. Furthermore, all of these are rather complex in themselves. Sensory restriction in one sense modality may or may not be a sufficient cause of disruption of a psychological process such as perception. What Hebb and his colleagues began was the enormous task of trying to specify just what it was in these situations which led to the changes in behavior. In other words, they set out to identify what aspects of these situations made them *stressful*.

The first of the experimental studies of sensory deprivation were performed at McGill University by Hebb's colleagues. They paid male college students twenty dollars per day to do *nothing!* All they had to do was to lie on a bed all day and night, with their eyes and hands covered, and all meaningful sounds masked off by a loud electric airconditioner. The subjects became upset. They hallucinated and had delusions. Their performance on various tests suffered, and generally they could tolerate the environment, or rather a lack of it, for only a couple of days. This was the first, the pioneering experiment in the area, and it is an extremely interesting piece of research. But we would like to concentrate on a study which was performed subsequent to the McGill research, one which manipulated sensory deprivation in a far more complete fashion.

In 1960, Jay T. Shurley, a professor of psychiatry at the University of Oklahoma School of Medicine, published a report termed, "Profound Experimental Sensory Isolation." The word "profound" is an apt description.

Shurley's definition of sensory isolation, that is, the experimental operation which he performed on the subjects, reduced the level of stimulation to as nearly absolute deprivation as seems possible (see Figure 1).

He had a special room-within-a-room constructed at the Oklahoma City Veterans Administration Hospital. In the interior room there was a well, lined with a thick layer of cork, and in that well was a tank, cut off from sources of vibration, sound or mechanical, in the outside world. The tank was filled with slowly flowing water maintained at a constant temperature, 93.5° Fahrenheit. The subject was suspended in the water. He was clad only in a mask which permitted him effortless breathing of pure, odor-free, constant-temperature air, and was instructed to inhibit body movement as much as was comfortably possible. Thus the subject was immersed in an environment which was as close as one can get to the total absence of stimulation. The subject experienced not only a uniform tactual field and unchanging temperature, but also had visual and auditory stimuli closed out by the tank and mask. The subject was given nothing to eat during his stay in the tank. His senses of taste, smell, touch, vision, and hearing were deprived of even remotely normal levels of stimulation. Furthermore, the mask was carefully weighted such that the subject's buoyancy was neutral, depriving him of normal

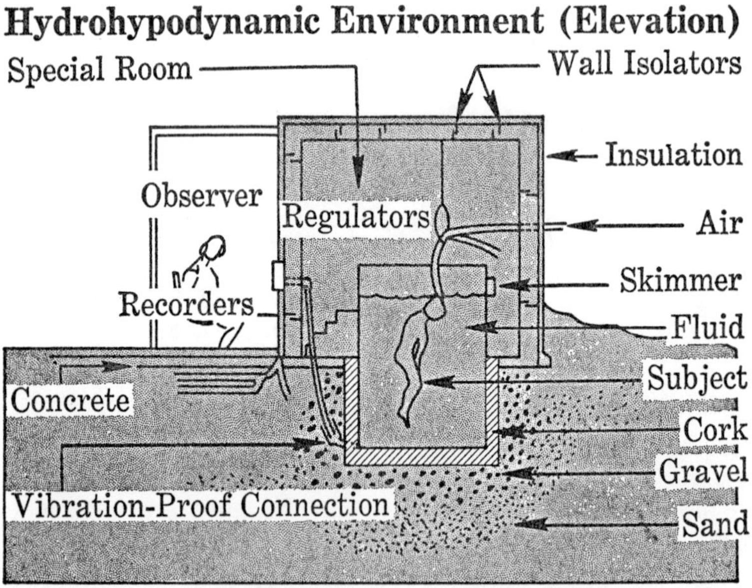

Hydrohypodynamic Environment (Elevation)

FIGURE 1. Schematic elevation of experimental sensory isolation laboratory.

gravity cues. All of the stimulation you constantly get from the muscles and joints of your body when you are walking, or when you are standing still maintaining an upright posture, were gone. Thus, Shurley created the situation which he used as the definition of sensory isolation.

What behaviors did he use to index personality change? Until this research we have considered experiments in which the investigators utilized a rather precise and narrow specification of some behavior which could be considered as defining personality change. Shurley simply observed and recorded what the subjects said. Some of them talked about their experiences as they were undergoing them, that is, into a microphone in the mask. Others gave reports from memory of what they had experienced in the tank. Full and open reporting was encouraged by absolute guarantees of anonymity. And so the subjects talked! They talked about what they "saw," what they "heard," and what they "felt."

No subject could endure the sensory deprivation for more than six hours. Paradoxically, all were willing to undergo the profound isolation again, despite the fact that their normal perceptual and intellectual functions were completely distorted. What Shurley called "mental imagery," subsuming dreams and hallucinations, occurred in the visual, auditory, kinesthetic (which means pertaining to stimulation from the muscles and tendons), and olfactory sense modalities. The best way to communicate in any real way how the subjects changed in the isolation condition is to do what Shurley did, that is, present a verbatim transcript of a part of a subject's report of an experimental session. The following is from a twenty-nine-year-old man, a journalist.

> In the second hour his comments concerned his self-thwarted, increasing urgency for "exercise" and physical activity; amazement at his lack of appetite for a cigarette; his state of utter loneliness and solitude, save for "my very real companions, my thoughts and memories"; compassion for the little space-monkey, Sam, who received only half an apple and a glass of water for his dinner after his historic trip 55 miles into space; thoughts of food and sudden, intense hunger pangs.
>
> He whistled, and then sang the refrain from a popular tune which went, "I'll never get rid of that ——, ——, ——!" Apparently he dropped off into a short (less than two minutes) nap; he woke with a start and the eerie feeling he had just been "out of this world," and with a very vivid, "long" dream, which he struggled to recall. He succeeded in recalling only a part—"a sawdust cream cone."
>
> In the third hour he questioned and then asserted he heard the very faint sound of water trickling (the tape records the sound); asserted he heard dogs barking (not present on the tape); and commented on a "crackling sound" (unable to verify from the tape). At intervals he sang, increasingly louder, the refrain from a slightly obscene ditty which began, "Roll me over . . ."
>
> Increasingly strong impulses to action came: "I had an urge to make like a porpoise, but those darned hoses

(air supply) won't let me!" Briefly, he seemed to be in quite an ebullient, elated mood. Suddenly, he plunged into grief and tears with the expressed thought, "How many people really think about what it's all about? How many people ever, ever think—just once—about love?"

Within seconds, the depressed mood vanished and he was again joking, whistling, and laughing. A make-believe dialogue ensued, as he asked, anxiously, "Joe, what do you do when your engine quits at 200 feet?" and replied, in a peal of laughter, "You land the sonofabitch!"

Immediately following, his tone shifted and he uttered an angry command: "You voice! Keep quiet up there! Quiet!" He, himself, obeyed, and was silent, but only briefly. He hummed. He sang. He sighed deeply. He yawned. He seemed unutterably bored.

His thoughts turned to his plan to compose his report and his budget, and the belated recognition he had not even begun to accomplish this. In a half-hearted explanation to himself, he said "I just allowed my thoughts to drift." Futility and resignation hung from his tone of voice. He then remarked briskly, "I seem kind of wide awake. I ought to get out!" For a period following this, there was more singing, more humming. Then, "I don't know, but it seems like I heard voices. Somewhere. Male voices. Men's voices. Too bad! (laughter) It should have been a bunch of dollies!" He laughed again. More singing came.

In a tone of extreme annoyance, he blurted out, "I might just as well be Sam, for all I can be or do or think or hear or be or smell or taste!"

Over the next 10 minutes he argued himself into the position that he was "just wasting time." "After all, I feel fine." "This is ridiculous" (here he referred to his being a grown man bobbing around in the dark in a tank of water in a hole under the hospital). "Besides," he added, "this run isn't producing any data for the doctor, anyway!"

Again, he commented and questioned whether he really was hearing "some noises." Abruptly, he pulled off the mask and left the tank. (pp. 541–542)

One female subject reported "seeing" several marvelous hallucinations, including a full-color, three-dimensional view of a "field of golden toadstools standing in bright sunlight." She also "saw" herself as an iced-tea spoon, slowly stirring a glass of iced tea. She woke up to find her left leg moving in a circular stirring motion! (Shurley, 1962). Other subjects reported seeing the experimenter through the walls of the tank, seeing patterns of brilliant lights, smelling garlic, smelling hot tar. One "heard" his name called by his father's voice. Other subjects reported unusual attentional effects. A physician reported hearing not only his heartbeat, but also the snapping shut of his aortic valve. Another physician reported "in awe" that he could hear the gliding sounds of his own skeletal joints as he moved. When the experimenter had to leave one subject for a few minutes, interrupting the postexperimental interview, he returned only to find the subject carrying on a rather animated interview of himself, both asking and answering questions.

There was, in short, a wide spectrum of alterations in the behavior of the sensorially isolated and deprived subjects.

Shurley set out with a question about "the nature and range of psychophysiological phenomena evoked in intact humans experimentally exposed in solitude to an environment which profoundly diminishes absolute amounts of sensory inputs . . ." (p. 539). He created such an environment and recorded what happened.

Shurley's study reflects a research strategy which involves asking a question almost at the level of the operations. It is a "what would happen if we did this" type of question, and very little reduction was involved in going from the original question to the research study itself. This is in sharp contrast to research like Hunt's, which began with a very theoretical question about the effects of frustration in infancy and wound up studying the hoarding behavior of rats.

While Shurley's question was at the level of operations, and involved relatively little reduction, it was asked in the context of a much broader question. How does brainwashing work? The research of Hebb, Shurley, and others, and the reports of former prisoners point to one important factor, sensory isolation.

EXPERIMENTAL NEUROSIS

You are all to some extent familiar with the term *neurosis*. In general, this term refers to mild-to-moderate problems in adjustment which are not usually serious enough to require hospitalization but which cause the sufferer and those around him a good deal of discomfort. In many textbooks neurosis or neurotic behavior is viewed as a reaction or set of reactions to stress. That is, in oversimplified terms, the person experiences some form of stress and in one way or another develops maladaptive behavior patterns which are termed neurotic.

There are many different definitions of "neurotic" behavior. However, there are some general forms of behavior which most psychologists would agree as characterizing neurosis. Behaviors which are not appropriate to the situation, which are very difficult to change, and which persist even in the face of punishment are usually labeled neurotic. For example, a person with the form of neurosis known as hysteria may develop a nonorganic paralysis and never walk again, even though such a neurosis may cost him his job and all opportunities for normal social interaction. The same is true of the person who so severely fears the opposite sex that he or she forms no heterosexual relationships even at the cost of being lonely and unhappy in a society largely oriented toward marriage and the family.

Psychiatrists and psychologists who work in hospitals, clinics, or private practice have long observed these kinds of behaviors. There have been many, many theories postulated over the years as to why neurotic people behave as they do. But these theories have been largely untested in the formal scientific sense. Our understanding of neuroses is far from complete. This aspect of human behavior is extremely difficult to study. Clearly we do not perform experimental manipulations on human subjects which may lead to persistent, maladaptive behavior. Furthermore, there are an extremely wide variety of behaviors defining neurosis and multitudes of factors that must be controlled if we are to take a research approach to the general question. Think for a moment about all of the things which may potentially be contributing factors in the development of neurotic behavior: child-rearing practices, socio-economic status, geographic area, genetic endowment, family size, constitutional sources like body build, and many more. Primarily because of these reasons, the animal laboratory has supplied most of the experimentally derived data aimed at clarifying the conditions under which these persistent and maladaptive responses develop. Of course, the experimenters have had to direct their research toward limited aspects of the problem. They have had to reduce this exceedingly complex issue to the point of asking narrow questions. As a consequence, the answers are also very limited in view of the magnitude of the "real-life" problem. The research to be discussed in the present section is an excellent example of this reducing process.

Experimenters have long observed that under certain

situations of laboratory-induced stress, animals manifested behavior which bore certain resemblances to human neurotic behavior. In fact, as long ago as the 1920's, a Russian physiologist, Ivan Pavlov, termed such behavior "experimental neurosis."

Researchers saw in these laboratory-produced animal behaviors the opportunity to examine ethically, under well-controlled laboratory conditions, the development of neurosis. The hope, of course, is that by understanding the development of behavior in this artificial setting, we might clarify some of the conditions under which human behavior disorders develop. Thus, for the past forty years or so, there have been numerous efforts to study the experimental neurosis, using a wide variety of animals as subjects.

As we have seen in the section discussing Hunt's research, Freud and his followers developed a theory of behavior which proposed that neurosis develops, at least in part, out of the traumatic experiences of childhood. Freud's theory is extremely elaborate, at times highly philosophical, and in general difficult to test experimentally. Nevertheless, some basic principles deriving from psychoanalytic thought have become extremely important in the experimental investigation of behavior. In 1943, a psychiatrist by the name of Jules H. Masserman published a book entitled *Behavior and Neurosis*. In this book he outlined some of these basic Freudian principles which guided his own study of experimental neurosis. The four basic principles, paraphrasing Masserman (pp. 7–8), are:

1. *Behavior is fundamentally motivated by the needs of the organism.* As Masserman points out, these needs may be termed "instincts" as in Freud's works, or "goal-directed striving," or whatever; the principle still holds.

2. *Behavior is contingent upon the demands of the environment and represents an adaptation between the individual and his changing surroundings.* This simply means that behavior is dependent upon interests, needs, and potentials and their interaction with the surroundings. Also implicit in this principle is the idea that between these two broad classes of determinants (the person and his environment), people in some way manage to form adaptive relationships with the world. He considers the environment (or in his terms, "milieu") to include stimuli from inside the body as well as cues and stimuli from outside.

3. *Behavior is not always a simple and direct satisfying of elementary needs.* Here Masserman is saying that basic phys-

iological drives become associated with many symbols and meanings and perhaps even other needs which are not physiological, and thus behavior includes thoughts, gestures, and words.

4. *The motivations of behavior may become conflicted when two or more needs are aroused at the same time and when the satisfaction of one of these needs necessarily prevents satisfaction of the others.* We have all experienced this state of affairs at least in relatively mild forms. For example, you want to have a rich dessert but you are already overweight. This last principle is the most important one for present purposes. Masserman argues that neurotic behavior results from the stress involved in experiencing conflicts between drives or needs. Masserman devotes a large portion of his book to a series of studies in which animals are subjected to different forms of conflict, and in which he describes the resultant changes in behavior.

Masserman presents the rationale for his experimental neurosis research program, and it will be helpful to outline his arguments. He points out that the basic principles summarized above lead directly to the manipulations necessary for laboratory investigations of experimental neurosis. That is, if the neurosis is based upon the conflict between two basic needs, then by following some rather simple procedures one has the ingredients of an experiment. Essentially the procedures are as follows:

1. *Producing or activating a strong biological drive.* For example, one could deprive an organism of food.

2. *Associating some stimulus with the conditions surrounding the satisfaction of that drive.* That is, one might present a tone to the organism just prior to feeding it.

3. *Placing the organism in conflict regarding the satisfaction of the drive.* Perhaps one might, at the time of reinforcement (food delivery), shock the animal, thus pitting fear and hunger against each other.

4. *Observing the effects of this conflict.* One would examine the organism's behavior at the time of conflict to see what adaptations it makes, but perhaps even more importantly, one would observe the organism's responses to the signal which has been associated with the conflict situation.

Masserman also points out that it is obviously important to select an animal species having the sensory and motor capacities necessary to carry out the responses and to make the associations required in these above situations. Therefore, he chose cats as subjects. Let us now examine, in some detail, a portion of his work.

Masserman manipulated the basic biological drive of hunger by depriving his cats of food. He then associated some stimulus with the satisfaction of the drive or, in this case, with the eating response. In order to do this, it was first necessary for Masserman to train his animals to make a specific response with which the stimulus could be associated. This was done by putting the hungry cat in a test cage containing a food box but no food. Food was then placed in the box and the subject was allowed to eat. Next, the signal (a light plus a bell) was given simultaneously with the placing of food in the box. After a series of such trials, animals quickly came to the food box and ate each time the signal was presented. Food was delivered *only* after the signal occurred.

The next step in the training of a specific response was to teach the animals to lift a lid on the food box to obtain food each time the signal was presented. This step was accomplished by lowering the lid on the box more and more as trials progressed. That is, each time the feeding signal was presented, the cats were required to increase their head contact with the box lid. Eventually the lid was completely closed and the cats had learned to lift the lid with their heads to get food in response to the signals. Essentially, the second major step had been accomplished; animals were associating the satisfaction of a drive with an external stimulus.

The third step necessary for the experiment was producing the conflict situation. This was done in three ways. After animals were trained to lift the food box lid and eat *in response to the light-bell signal* some were subjected to an aversive air-blast just at the moment of feeding. Others received shock through the floor of the cage just as they began to eat. Still others received a combination of blast and shock right at this crucial time. Thus, Masserman argued that he was pitting two needs against one another, (1) the drive to eat and (2) the need to avoid or escape the noxious stimulation. Conflict-induced stress has now been added to the situation. If it is correct that this type of stress produces the experimental neurosis, then the behavior of these cats should show marked changes and these changes should be persistent and maladaptive. Here, maladaptive refers to behaviors which interfere with the satisfaction of the drive to eat.

Masserman points out that there were extremely wide individual differences in the ways in which his cats reacted. In general, however, he was able to categorize the behavior changes into four types of reactions: (1) changes in spontaneous activity, (2) "phobic" responses to feeding signals, (3) "counterphobic" behavior patterns, and (4) "regressive" behavior. Let us examine two of these categories of neurotic behavior more closely.

1. *Changes in spontaneous activity.* Masserman noted that animals which were generally quiet and not very active in the feeding situation became "restless or agitated" after being subjected to the conflict. For example, "cat 53 was a normally quiet animal in which two blasts of air abolished further feeding responses but produced a fidgety, incessant pacing and shifting from side to side . . . and characteristic postures and acting . . . (which mimicked) anxiety" (p. 67). On the other hand, animals which were generally active during the feeding situation became remarkably quiet and passive. "Cats 14 and 52 were highly excitable and easily distractible animals, which reacted with frenzied leaping at the air-blasts but which thereafter refused to feed with food easily available and lay passive and immobile between feeding signals in any portion of the cage in which they were placed" (p. 67). Another normally active cat appeared to go to sleep after only two shock experiences.

2. *"Phobic" responses to the feeding signals.* One fairly common human neurotic reaction is to become "phobic." That is, to develop fears centering around specific objects or situations in the environment. The reader has probably heard of claustrophobia, the fear of closed places, or acrophobia, the fear of heights, and other phobias. Some of Masserman's cats developed responses to the feeding signals that seemed to parallel what we observe when people who suffer from phobias are in proximity to the feared object or situation. Animals which normally rushed to the food box following the feeding signal now responded to the stimuli by crouching, hiding, attempting to escape the cage, and by showing extreme signs of anxiety or fear. They trembled and appeared to panic. In some cases these responses lasted for months even in the absence of air-blasts or shocks.

It is clear from these findings that Masserman's cats did develop persistent and maladaptive responses and that, in this sense, these behaviors could be termed neurotic. The question is, however, were these responses really due to the conflict engendered, or would these neurotic behaviors occur as a function of the other operations involved in the experiment? That is, could the presentation of the light-bell stimulus itself produce the changes? Could a simple pairing of these stimuli with air blasts "cause" a neurosis? Clearly, these and other questions had to be answered before the experimental neurosis operations could be interpreted unambiguously. Therefore, Masserman carried out a series of control experiments.

1. *Will cats develop a neurosis as a function of experiencing the light-bell signal alone?* Cats were exposed to the light-bell signal but no food reward was associated with the stimulus. At first, animals were startled by the signal but soon they ignored it. No experimental neurosis developed.

2. *Will air-blasts plus the light-bell signal produce the behavior changes?* Cats were subjected to the light-bell stimulus paired with air-blasts. At first, fear responses such as cowering and trembling developed to the signal. However, these rapidly diminished and then disappeared. Also, signals given during feeding failed to produce any observable effect. Again, no experimental neurosis. Up to now, no conflict, no neurosis.

3. *Will the air-blast itself produce experimental neurosis?* Masserman exposed cats to air-blasts at irregular intervals in the absence of any signal. The subjects rapidly became accustomed to this stimulation and soon showed no disturbed behavior except when the blast occurred. Again, no conflict, no neurosis.

4. *Will experimental neurosis develop as a function of feeding frustration?* Cats were trained to lift the food box lid and eat in response to the light-bell signal. Then Masserman presented the signal but locked the food box. The animals soon abandoned the food-seeking response and no neurosis appeared.

5. *Will irregular food rewards "cause" a neurosis?* Animals were first trained to eat in response to the signal. They were then rewarded (given food in the food box) only some of the time. These operations also failed to produce neurotic behavior.

Masserman carried out other control experiments investigating different kinds of frustrations as well as factors such as the possible effects of constricting animals in small spaces. In no case did he produce the neurotic behaviors observed in the experiments involving conflict.

The above mentioned control experiments strongly support Masserman's argument that it is the conflictual aspect of the experimental situation which is the major determinant of the observed neurosis. However, this is only part of the story. Masserman also asked the question: Given the development of this abnormal behavior, is it possible to give these cats "psychotherapy" and eliminate the neurosis? He conducted six experiments to examine the conditions under which the persistent, maladaptive behavior patterns may be eliminated. Let us examine three of these.

1. Thirty-seven neurotic cats were returned to the experimental situation after *rest periods* varying from two weeks to five months following the development of the neurosis. Thirty of these animals demonstrated neurotic behavior which was just as severe as was present on the last day of the neurosis-producing operations.

2. A second therapeutic procedure which Masserman employed was the *"reduction of one of the conflictual drives."* Those neurotic cats which were force-fed just before being returned to the experimental cage usually showed significant reductions in neurotic behavior when the feeding signal was presented. It is important to note, however, that it was not possible to reinstate the normal feeding response to the light-bell signal when animals were placed in the test cage hungry. In fact, as soon as the hunger drive was reestablished, the cats again displayed neurotic behavior in response to the feeding signal.

3. Another attempt to provide psychotherapy for the neurotic animals was to *place a normal cat in the experimental situation with a neurotic one*. Each neurotic subject was put into the test cage with a nonneurotic cat trained to eat to the feeding signal. The results of these operations were only partially successful. In some cases the behavior of the nonneurotic animals eventually led to the neurotic subject's eating in response to the signal. In some cases normal behavior was reinstated. In other cases, the neurotic cat ate in response to the signal only hesitantly and irregularly, while still other neurotic animals failed to reestablish the normal eating response even after numerous trials over a two-week period.

While it is apparent that Masserman was able to effect some "cures" by instituting procedures aimed at reducing the basic conflict involved, in no case was treatment 100 percent effective. The therapeutic procedures were more effective than the rest-period operation, that is, more effective than no therapy at all. He stated that those treatments which were aimed at reducing or abolishing conflict were the most successful.

Masserman presents data which indicate that the best therapy may be starving the animal and placing the cat within sight and smell of the food. This has the effect of reducing the conflict because the hunger drive becomes so much stronger than the tendency to avoid the food box. He also points out that a combination of therapies would probably be best for any one neurotic cat.

What does this research have to say about our original question: Why does a person's personality change under stress? Masserman has demonstrated that certain systematic behavioral changes in cats, which he calls "neurotic," result from conflict between motives. It has been pointed out several times already, that such a demonstration allows us to look for similar relationships in situations where experimental manipulations are impossible. It should also be pointed out, however, what this set of experiments has *not* demonstrated. It has not demonstrated that the kinds of changes recorded are the *only* ones. They are the ones that the investigator focused upon. Nor has it been demonstrated that *only* conflict will lead to the kinds of changes noted. The investigator has ruled out other aspects of his experiment which might have led to the experimental neurosis. There may be a wide variety of other sources of experimental neurosis, which he did not have in his situation. Finally, the study did not show the actual mechanism, if one can be shown, whereby conflict leads to the overt behavioral changes.

While Masserman's research with cats suggests what to look for in studying human neurosis, it has not *demonstrated* that conflict is a factor in the development of neurosis in people.

A PSYCHOPHYSIOLOGICAL APPROACH TO STRESS

We have seen that stresses of different kinds lead to a variety of behavioral alterations in men and animals alike. Sometimes the behavioral alterations produced in laboratories are maladaptive, manifest themselves outside of the actual experimental situation, and persist after the stress is no longer being applied. These, as we have seen, are labeled *experimental neuroses*. Masserman's research provides one of the best known examples of experimental neurosis, but there are many, many others. Sheep, dogs, goats, rats, pigs, and primates, as well as cats, have been employed as experimental subjects. Behavioral changes have run the gamut from minute, localized responses such as facial twitches (or tics) to wholesale personality changes in the animals. An example of such major changes would be the "suspiciousness" Howard S. Liddell (1954) found in his experimental sheep. The usually very gregarious animals actually refused to join the flock after they had been subjected to the stress situations employed in that particular study.

The experimental neurosis literature deals with a question of potentially great significance: *What are the essential conditions leading to the lasting disturbances in behavior we call "experimental neurosis"?* If we can specify them in the laboratory, then perhaps we'll know where to look in that enormously complex arena, real life, for the conditions giving rise to actual human neurosis. This is, of course, the credo of the laboratory investigator. Let us examine several ways of approaching the question just posed.

This area of research is defined by the common effects that the different experimental neurosis manipulations have on organisms. That is, the area is defined by behavior disturbances meeting the criterion for being labeled neurotic.

One tactic which someone might wish to employ would be to examine the various experimental designs very carefully, and to try to abstract from them some common element. The next step would be to design studies employing this particular manipulation and ruling out alternative explanations.

The obvious example to present here is Masserman, who considered the crucial manipulations to be those which engendered conflict in the organism. Other investigators have abstracted other common elements from the literature and have suggested that it is not conflict that is crucial, but fear or anxiety. A major problem is that these terms are closely related, and it is difficult to set up experimental situations in which one is present and the others are completely ruled out or controlled. Perhaps this problem, which is in part a definitional one, could be overcome by adopting a slightly different tactic. Perhaps, instead of performing the experimental neurosis manipulations, observing the neuroses, and inferring the construct (conflict, fear, etc.), there might be a better theoretical payoff in looking for something which is apparently common to all of the constructs which have been postulated, in proposing an alternative construct representing this common process, and in trying to measure that construct.

Harold J. Johnson, now at Bowling Green State University, has proposed such an alternative formulation regarding the development of experimental neurosis (Johnson, 1963). In reviewing the literature he was impressed with the fact that while many of the experiments would engender fear or anxiety through the use of shock, there were many others which did not employ any operation which would normally be considered fear or anxiety provoking. There were many studies in which no noxious stimulation was used.

One of the major methods employed engenders conflict

by presenting subjects with a difficult sensory discrimination task.

In this technique the animal might be put into a situation in which it is presented two different but similar stimuli on different trials. As an example, let us assume that circles and ellipses are presented in a random sequence. The animal is rewarded with food for responding to a circle. But if it does not respond to that circle, it is not rewarded. Conversely, on other trials, it would be presented an ellipse and would be rewarded for not making a response, but not rewarded for responding. In such a procedure there seems to be no operation which is fear or anxiety provoking.

Johnson's proposed alternative formulation was in terms of a construct which had found wide usage in the study of motivation, the construct of *arousal*. In his words: "It is suggested here that the use of such terms as fear and anxiety do not adequately describe the phenomenon [of experimental neurosis] and that the evidence is more clearly understood if one thinks in terms of physiological arousal rather than in terms of anxiety or fear which imply some real or perceived threat to the organism" (p. 116).

It is his contention that all of the experimental manipulations used in experimental neurosis research bring about high levels of physiological arousal, which "eventually result in the breakdown of the animal" (p. 115). Arousal, as used in this context, refers to a construct having a variety of behavioral referents. For example, the individual who is highly aroused may be extremely alert, or if too highly aroused, he may be so tense and overresponsive that he behaves inappropriately in many situations. Highly aroused persons may appear to be very anxious or disorganized. The construct of arousal was originally derived from physiological research, and it is often indexed by such measures as heart rate, brain waves, respiration rate, skin conductance, and so forth. These measures of physiological functioning which can be taken from *outside* the organism, and which the investigator is attempting to relate to behaviors such as those mentioned above, are called *psychophysiological measures*. The overall goal of Johnson's research can be seen as an attempt to relate the construct of arousal to experimental neurosis.

The concrete goal of this particular study is narrower still. Johnson designed an experiment to show that one specific effect of one typical experimental neurosis manipulation was a change in certain measures commonly regarded as indices of physiological arousal. Specifically, his intent was to "demonstrate the existence of high levels of arousal brought about by difficult discrimination tasks" (p. 116).

As we look closely at his study, keep in mind that he

hoped to get some evidence for his contention that arousal was the key factor in the development of experimental neurosis.

The subjects were sixty female students in an introductory psychology course. While they were required to participate in a number of experiments as a part of the course, the only students who served in this experiment were those who agreed to do so after a one-second test shock, which was the same strength and duration used throughout the experiment. The subjects were divided into four groups, two of which would be considered "experimental" and two "control." All of the subjects participated for three 50-minute sessions, during which continuous recordings were made of their heart rates, skin conductances, and palmar sweat (the latter two being measures of perspiration). At this point we will describe in detail the operations defining the four groups.

DIFFICULT DISCRIMINATION GROUP. Each of the fifteen subjects in this first experimental group was seated in a comfortable chair and hooked up to the recording apparatus by various recording electrodes. A subject rested an index finger on a lever and had a shock electrode taped to that index finger. Her task in the first of the three sessions was to respond to a signal, a two-second presentation of a metronome beating at 144 beats per minute, by lifting her finger off the switch. If she failed to respond, she got a mild shock. If, however, the two-second metronome signal was at a frequency of 60 beats per minute, she would get shocked if she *lifted* her finger, but would avoid shock by keeping her finger where it was. Or, in diagram form,

FAST BEAT	LIFT	NO SHOCK
FAST BEAT	NO LIFT	SHOCK
SLOW BEAT	LIFT	SHOCK
SLOW BEAT	NO LIFT	NO SHOCK

In the second session the same procedure was used, except that during the session the slow beat was made faster and faster until it became similar enough to the fast beat that the subjects began making errors. In other words, they had difficulty discriminating between the two beats. In the third session, the discrimination problem remained very difficult for the subjects, except for the last five trials. These last five were made very easy so that subjects would not leave the experiment in an agitated state.

IMPOSSIBLE DISCRIMINATION GROUP. This group was treated in the same way as the difficult discrimination group for the first two sessions. In the third session, however, the treatment of the two experimental groups diverged. The discrimination was made impossible for this group, by increasing the speed of the slow beat to 144 beats per minute! On some of the trials, the experimenter considered the 144-beat stimulus to be the fast one, and punished the failure to respond. On the other trials, he considered the 144 to be the slow beat and punished the responses.

CONTROL GROUPS. To rule out the possibility that any changes in arousal occurring over the course of the experiment may have been due to the effect of shock in and of itself, a group of subjects was yoked to the difficult discrimination group. This means that each subject in this control group was paired with a subject in the difficult discrimination group and heard a 144 beat tone as often as her counterpart in the experimental group, but she never heard the other tone. She also got a shock every time her counterpart got one. The subjects in this control group were therefore unable to discriminate between shock and nonshock trials. In order to eliminate any possibility that changes in arousal might be due simply to the effects of unpredictability of shock another control group was employed. Subjects in the other groups were unable to predict without error when they would get shocked. Therefore, each subject in this second control group was yoked to a subject in the impossible discrimination group, and got shocked as often as did her experimental counterpart. This control group, however, heard the 144-beat signal *only* on those occasions prior to receiving shock. Thus, there was no uncertainty aroused by the signal; when they heard it they knew that they were about to get shocked. And they never got shocked without a signal.

The control groups, then, were treated identically with the experimental groups except that neither of the control groups could avoid shock by discriminating appropriately between signals, and the second control group had no uncertainty about when shock would occur. Notice that there has been a great emphasis placed upon controlling for the effects of shock. There is a very important reason for this. Since Johnson was interested in studying arousal as a function of difficult discrimination, he had to pay particular attention to any other factors which might produce arousal. Shock is a potent source of arousal.

As you will see, another way to conceptualize the function of the control subjects in this experiment is as a base line group with which to compare whatever changes may occur in the experimental subjects.

In this particular experiment the analysis of the results, the heart rates, and sweat and conductance data is made particularly difficult by several considerations. It happened that the original levels on these measures were quite different from group to group. This makes any simple comparisons between the groups essentially uninterpretable. In addition to the different starting points, there is another major problem. It is well known among investigators who use these psychophysiological measures that the subject gets used to the experiment and to whatever stimulation he is receiving. The psychophysiological measures gradually habituate, that is, they return slowly to a point close to their "normal" level. Since the effects of habituation are in the opposite direction of the expected effects of the experimenter's manipulation, the crucial evaluation of the data is a test of whether or not the groups *change differently* over the course of the experiment. In fact, the groups did change differentially over time in the experiment. The heart rate scores remained about the same for the experimental groups, increasing slightly overall, but increasing fairly sharply from session two to session three. Conversely, the heart rates of the control groups decreased over the course of the experiment. Therefore, the requirement that the subjects make difficult or impossible discriminations to avoid shock had a greater effect on the psychophysiology of the organism, specifically on the heart rate, than did an equivalent amount of shock alone. Very similar results were found with the skin conductance and the palmar sweat measures. The statistical analyses of the data showed that the groups changed differently over time, or, in more technical terms, the effect of time on the psychophysiological measures was dependent upon the nature of the experimental manipulations. The two sources of change in the measure of behavior *interacted*. A study of the graphs presented in Johnson's report of his research reveals that the experimental subjects responded differently from the controls, and the major difference occurred between the second and third sessions. The control groups continued to display a decrease in arousal. The experimental subjects, especially the impossible discrimination group, increased most at that point.

Johnson also collected some other information by conducting postexperimental interviews. The results of the analyses on the data collected in this way were in agreement with the results of the analyses of the psychophysiological data.

Johnson sums up his interpretation of his results as follows: "All of the results of this study seem to indicate that the effects of experimental neurosis paradigms might best be phrased in terms of increases in physiological arousal rather than in terms of fear or anxiety responses" (p. 123).

Let's back up now, and see precisely what this experiment accomplished. First, let's consider a specific point which is primarily of interest as an aside, then let's try to place this study, now completed, back in the context of answering a larger question.

The more specific issue deals with an interesting comparison between two of the groups. Look back at the operations for the third session for the impossible discrimination group. Compare them with the first control group discussed. They are identical. Both groups heard only the 144-beat tone, both were able to move their finger off the key, but both were, in fact, helpless. The delivery or nondelivery of the shocks were beyond their control. Yet, their behavior was radically different, as measured psychophysiologically. If an observer were trying to make sense out of the experimental operations and had only the third session to examine, he would have a hopeless task. What was different about these two groups in the third session? Only one thing was different, their own history, and therefore, what they were trying to do. The subjects in the impossible discrimination group brought to session three a two-session history of success in avoiding shock. They had learned that they could control what was going to happen by making the appropriate responses to the noticeably different stimuli. The control subjects, however, had right from the outset of the experiment been completely unable to exert any control over whether they would get shocked or not. In essence, they were not trying. Any interpretation of experimental results must always take into account what the *subject* is trying to do in the experimental situation. A moment's reflection on the research performed by Miller on the acquisition, or learning, of fear, will suffice to reinforce this point. Whether or not a situation is stressful for a given organism will very likely depend upon the history of that organism.

Now let's place the study back into the context of the larger question. While Johnson's broad purpose was to isolate a crucial factor underlying the development of experimental neurosis, if we stick to the level of the data, he demonstrated that forcing a human female subject to make difficult discriminations to avoid shock had a rather great influence on several measures of arousal. This study is a made-to-order example of what was said earlier about taking a question and breaking it down into answerable pieces. It is but one small step in the direction of establishing with any certainty that arousal is actually a key construct in the development of experimental neurosis. What would have to be done further to establish that contention? First, all of the experimental operations which lead to experimental neurosis would have to be investigated in a similar manner. It would have to be demonstrated that all of them do in fact result in high levels of physiological arousal. It would then have to be demonstrated that, under some conditions, high levels of physiological arousal will ultimately lead to the kinds of sustained behavioral alterations which define experimental neurosis. Note well that this was *not* demonstrated in the study just reported. Also note the implication that arousal need not lead to experimental neurosis under all conditions. There may be other conditions which channel the effects of arousal toward some other form of behavioral change. In sum, in order to firmly establish the relationship between arousal and experimental neurosis, the conditions under which arousal does and does not lead to experimental neurosis would have to be carefully and completely delineated.

Johnson's experiment was one, carefully designed step in a very long, involved process. If the relation between stress and experimental neurosis could be clarified in terms of arousal by the very large number of equally carefully designed studies which would be required, we would still have the question of relevance to human neurosis produced outside the laboratory.

VOODOO DEATH

Up to now we have focused upon laboratory experimentation as the mode by which researchers have attempted to answer questions regarding the relationships between stress and behavior changes. Generally, these investigators have, in one way or another, attempted to manipulate conditions in a careful fashion and to quantify their results as much as possible. We have seen how elaborate control operations have been constructed and how experimenters have attempted to rule out, as much as possible, alternative explanations of their findings.

We are now going to examine a bit of research which in the formal experimental sense does none of these things and yet in one way or another does many of them. We are going to see how a researcher, W. B. Cannon (1942), has attempted to utilize data from observers of numerous cultures plus the hard data from the laboratory to interpret a fascinating phenomenon, "voodoo" death.

For centuries, students of so-called primitive cultures have observed and recorded deaths which on the surface appear to be caused by black magic. These voodoo deaths have occurred in various parts of the world: South America, South Africa, Australia, New Zealand, Haiti, and the Pacific Islands.

The magical means by which they are accomplished take various forms. In some areas if a native discovers he has eaten a taboo, but not physically poisonous, food, he may die very soon afterward. In other areas if a person hears that a death curse has been placed upon him by a witch or shaman, the voodoo death occurs. In other cases if a magician points a certain kind of bone at his victim, the victim literally wastes away and dies within a matter of days.

These are recorded "facts." A particularly good description of such events is given by Cannon, who quotes an on-the-spot observer of this phenomenon, Dr. Herbert Basedow, a student of primitive Australian cultures. Dr. Basedow states:

> The man who discovers that he is being boned by any enemy is, indeed, a pitiable sight. He stands aghast, with his eyes staring at the treacherous pointer, and with his hands lifted as though to ward off the lethal medium, which he imagines is pouring into his body. His cheeks blanch and his eyes become glassy and the expression of his face becomes horribly distorted . . . he attempts to shriek but usually the sound chokes in his throat, and all that one might see is froth at his mouth. His body begins to tremble and the muscles twist involuntarily. He sways backwards and falls to the ground, and after a short time appears to be in a swoon but soon after he writhes as if in mortal agony, and, covering his face with his hands begins to moan. After a while he becomes very composed and crawls to his wurley. From this time onwards he sickens and frets, refusing to eat and keeping aloof from the daily affairs of the tribe. Unless help is forthcoming in the shape of a countercharm administered by the hands of the Nangarri, or medicine-man, his death is only a matter of a comparatively short time. If the coming of the medicine-man is opportune he might be saved (p. 172).

The course of events is fairly similar from place to place. The individual who has been cursed is convinced he will die, as are his enemies, friends, and relatives alike. He isolates himself from his social environment, and as we shall see, people in his environment systematically isolate him. He stops eating and drinking, and in a matter of a few days he is dead.

To the majority of us this may seem impossible. It is against everything we have been taught to believe. Since childhood most of us are told that there are no such things as witches and that magic is only make-believe. It is fairly common knowledge that magicians in our culture are really master tricksters. But if this is true, how can we explain or understand voodoo death? One question immediately comes to mind. Are voodoo deaths in reality nothing more than deaths by natural causes? We know from the anthropological literature that primitive cultures tend to try and make their world safer and more understandable by creating what seems to us to be strange explanations of natural phenomena. Perhaps disease, old age, or willful starvation may in fact explain these mysterious mortalities. Perhaps they are due to poison. If Cannon were constructing a traditional experiment, these two general questions would have to be answered by using control operations. This was not possible. But he tried to achieve the functions of control, that is, he tried to rule out the above-stated, obvious, possible explanations of such events. How did he accomplish this? First of all, the possibility that old age is the most important determinant is ruled out by the fact that many victims were described as "young," "robust," and "strong." Starvation is ruled out by the rapidity with which death occurs. But how about disease as a major contributing factor? Here the evidence is quite hard. Medical examinations of victims (when available) revealed no physical cause of death. Likewise, available postmortem examinations revealed no physical cause of death. These findings also answer, in part, the question about death by poisoning. In addition, it was often reported by observers that in many of the cultures in which the voodoo deaths occurred people were ignorant of the use of poison. In other cases, there were very few poisons available. With these obvious explanations ruled out, then, the question is, can we find some scientifically acceptable reason for these events? Magic is not acceptable. Most scientists believe that explanations based on magic, witchcraft, the supernatural, are really just ways of saying that we don't understand. It does seem clear that something psychological is going on. There is a recorded case in which the witch had been forced to tell his victim that it was all a mistake, whereupon the unfortunate person suddenly got well. Other cases like this support at least a partial psychological explanation of voodoo death.

How did Cannon go about determining just what psychological processes were operating? His first step was to try to discover under what general conditions the voodoo deaths occur. He was able to point to a couple of common factors. First of all, voodoo deaths are reported in extremely backward, superstitious, and fear-ridden cultures. These are cultures in which the levels of education and technology are so very primitive that it is quite possible for a member to believe without a doubt that someone could actually kill him by pointing a bone at him.

Secondly, it appears to be common that once the individual has been doomed the people around him go through a two-stage social process. First of all, they withdraw *all* social support. They change all their attitudes toward him. He is now considered taboo, or perhaps sacred, but he is certainly *not* considered to be a normal person. The individual victim is in a totally new and threatening situation. He is isolated. He is no longer a member of the social group. He is *alone*. This, in and of itself, is an extremely stress-provoking situation, particularly in primitive cultures where life itself is often dependent upon one's relationships with kinsmen and tribal members.

In the second stage of this social process, the people around him begin to treat the victim as if he were already dead. He is mourned and he mourns himself.

Thus, the victim is in a social situation where deaths due to magic are as believable to him as deaths due to automobile accidents are to us. But is the belief that an event can cause death really enough to kill someone when the event occurs? This is not a completely satisfactory answer. Something else must cause the actual physical death. What?

Cannon has been an important figure in the area of physiology and particularly in the physiology of emotional behavior. It was thus quite normal that he should turn to this level of investigation to look for an answer. He asked the question: Is it possible for intense fear to actually kill?

Here Cannon leaned heavily upon *previous* laboratory research to help him answer the question. He said that we know from past research that emotional arousal has profound effects upon physiological activity. The so-called sympathetic nervous system is highly involved in bodily functioning and affects the operation of major internal organs like the heart, respiratory system, blood vessels, etc. Relatively long-term, intense, sympathetic functioning can clearly have "dire results," as Cannon put it.

In addition to this general knowledge, from the results of animal research, Cannon knew that it might be possible that death could occur in a matter of hours under conditions of intense emotional stress. In fact, researchers suggest that the extreme bodily responses observed in these kinds of deaths are much like those observed in the state of physiological shock attending physical injury. One major aspect of this type of shock is a drastic drop in blood pressure which is often fatal to humans.

Thus, Cannon concluded, it is quite possible that intense fear can in fact produce death. Now, how did this help Cannon arrive at a meaningful and scientifically acceptable answer to voodoo death? If fear can lead to death, then it is at least possible that the voodoo victim literally dies of fright.

This statement becomes much more meaningful if we return to the social conditions in which the victim is immersed. Remember, he believes unquestioningly that bone pointing or other magic will kill him, as does everyone around him. He is treated as if he were dead and he treats himself in the same way.

These conditions must be an extreme source of stress. This should be apparent if you think for a minute about how drastically your beliefs and the opinions of others can affect your emotional state. But the initial and very potent source of terror comes from simply finding out that one has been pointed at. If the reader doubts this, he should reread the quote above relating the response of a victim upon discovering that he'd been cursed. It seems very reasonable to assume that all of the social conditions are such that intense fear plays a major role in voodoo deaths. We might view the sequence in the following simplified manner: (1) The profound belief in the possibility of death by magic, which is reinforced by the victim's environment, leads to (2) an intense state of fear that produces (3) profound physiological changes leading to a state of severe physiological shock, (4) severe drops in blood pressure, and finally (5) death. The fact that most observers report that the subject fails to eat or drink probably contributes to the rapid demise.

Cannon studied this phenomenon outside of the laboratory, but his study is by no means just speculation. Cannon gathered his data thoroughly; he evaluated alternative explanations; he utilized sound research findings and from these "operations" deduced a scientifically acceptable and logical explanation. But Cannon was not so naïve as to believe that he had proven his contention. In fact, he pointed out that his conclusions were really nothing more than logically derived hypotheses, and that there were operations one could perform in order to test his notions. Workers should attempt to obtain definitive physiological measures from voodoo victims, measures that would provide direct evidence of the presence or absence of physiological shock attending these occurrences.

Beyond providing us with a meaningful hypothesis and a method for testing it, what else has Cannon done? First of all, he's provided some very interesting data regarding human behavior, in addition to any attempts to understand it. Secondly, as we have seen, he has attempted to make scientific sense out of a phenomenon which is exceedingly difficult to comprehend. Thirdly, he has to some extent demonstrated the tremendous potency of belief systems and how they may affect behavior. External events (for example, bone pointing) plus the past experience of the organism may produce behavioral changes that are almost unbelievable. In this sense he has said something we already know, but he has said so in a very powerful manner. It's not just the particular external event that produces stress, but it is the event plus whatever meaning the event has for the individual. If an acquaintance pointed a bone at you and said you would therefore die, you wouldn't drop dead. You would probably laugh at him.

While it may seem that Cannon's work is completely different from the research so far discussed, a bit of reflection may show this to be untrue. Other investigators have taken generally large questions and have reduced them to the level of laboratory operations in attempts to provide a partial answer. Cannon has also taken on a very large question. He has not reduced it by developing his own operations in an effort to provide the answer. He has, however, gone through this reductionistic process. Part of his analysis was at the level of blood pressure drops in animals. He selected relevant research evidence that others had already provided through operations in the laboratory. In this way the process of reduction was carried out in spite of the fact that Cannon did not do a specific experiment aimed at this specific question.

BEHAVIOR MODIFICATION

The voodoo death section presented a rather marked shift from preceding ones with respect to the methods used by the investigator. Cannon took a complex social phenomenon and interpreted it in terms of generally well-understood physiological phenomena.

The present chapter presents a marked shift as well. But this shift is of a very different sort, involving a philosophy of research divergent in some respects from anything we have thus far presented. In fact, it represents a philosophy of research which does not fit neatly or completely into the discussion of science that we presented in Part I of this volume.

The study which we will discuss in this section was done in the tradition of one of the best known of American psychologists, B. F. Skinner. The Skinnerian tradition represents a departure from the model of science presented, but not with respect to what we have described as its essential feature, the emphasis on repeatable, controlled observations and clearly defined manipulations. In fact, Skinner and his followers stress the importance of observables even more. The essential difference between the Skinnerian framework and the one in which we have been proceeding thus far lies in their respective attitudes toward hypothetical constructs and formal theorizing. The model we have presented in Part I and have exemplified in Part II thus far has as its goal the *understanding* of behavior in the sense of postulating useful theoretical constructs. Skinner and his colleagues are not concerned with the postulation and elucidation of these underlying, inferred processes. Rather, they have set for themselves the goal of trying to describe the *contingencies* under which behavior can be systematically and predictably controlled. The use of the word *control* in the Skinnerian framework is very different from the way we have used it so far. Up until now, control has had the meaning of experimental control, the aspect of research design by which we rule out possible explanations of the data other than the one in which we are interested. Skinner's use is a more literal one. By control he means having—and using—a thorough knowledge of the stimulus conditions which regulate and direct the behavior of organisms. The basic stimulus conditions which Skinner has dedicated his scientific career to investigating are the rewards and punishments which follow immediately upon responses and which have such a profound effect on subsequent responses and the stimuli which precede them. Skinner's operant techniques, as well as techniques of other experimental psychologists, are finding their way out of the animal laboratory and into the classroom and clinic. This section addresses the application of these techniques to a major aspect of clinical psychology, the modification of abnormal behavior.

Why are the laboratory methods used in investigating the behavior of lower organisms, primarily of rats and pigeons, coming into clinical use? There are many reasons. We will discuss four.

1. *The lack of success of diagnostic approaches in leading to specific treatment programs.* One of the standard functions of the psychologist or psychiatrist interested in treating the mentally ill has been diagnosis. The first step, much as it is in medicine, has been to diagnose the patient, to identify the "disease." Diagnosis in medicine, however, has direct consequences in terms of a specified set of treatment operations which the diagnosis leads the medical practitioner to employ. In clinical psychology the diagnosis and treatment are not nearly so closely related. Diagnosis may not be completely unrelated to specific psychotherapeutic treatment, but many would argue that as it is used it certainly does not necessarily point the way to a specific set of therapeutic operations. Rewording this in terms of this book, diagnostic procedures often do not isolate the effects of stress on personality in a definite enough way to indicate specific treatment.

2. *The lack of adequate direction by personality theory.* Closely related to the above is the failure of personality theory to provide direction in psychotherapy. Practitioners of differ-

ent schools speak very different theoretical languages. However, there have been investigators who have studied what goes on in psychotherapy who have claimed that therapists' behavior when actually doing therapy with a patient is virtually independent of the theoretical language spoken. These investigators have also noted that as therapists of different schools gain experience, their methods of treatment become less and less related to their theoretical explanations of what they are doing, and more and more similar to each other's treatment methods. To be sure, many practitioners of psychotherapy would strongly dispute this point. Again in terms of this book, the current theories of personality are so vague about statements of the relationship between specific forms of stress and psychological symptoms that *specific* treatment procedures cannot readily be deduced from the theories.

3. *The lack of demonstrable success of psychotherapy itself.* Research dealing with the extent to which psychotherapy is successful is extraordinarily difficult to do. One problem is the measurement of improvement. Another is the base-rate problem, that is, many of the patients who improve under therapy may have done so *without* any special treatment. What research has been done suggests that with mildly disturbed, neurotic patients, the traditional methods lead to improvement only about as often as would be expected if you left the patient alone. With respect to severely disturbed patients there is disagreement among psychotherapists as to the effectiveness of treatment.

4. *The desire to bring the findings of the laboratory into practical use.* In addition to the negative reasons given above, there is a powerful positive motive for bringing Skinnerian techniques, and other experimental techniques, into the clinic. Many laboratory scientists are not only anxious to test their findings outside the laboratory for theoretical purposes, but are also impatient to see some immediate, socially relevant results of their research.

While the application of these laboratory-based techniques to problems of behavior disturbance is relatively new, and the goals of the applications are frequently limited, what evidence there is is really exciting. While the case history we present below is in the Skinnerian tradition, we would like to make it clear to the reader that there are now many other laboratory-based approaches to the modification of deviant behavior, producing equally dramatic and equally exciting results.

Instead of trying to answer the question, Why does a

person's personality change under stress? the therapist with a Skinnerian orientation will say something like, "There may be antecedent stressful conditions for that disturbed behavior I see in that particular individual. I choose not to ask why he is behaving that way, but rather I choose to *change* his behavior by appropriate rewards and punishments." This does not mean that such a therapist avoids doing an assessment of the person. In a very general sense he makes a diagnosis. But this process does not involve labeling the "disease" or talking about underlying personality dynamics. Rather, the assessment involves detailing the problem behavior, identifying the stimulus conditions that give rise to it, and observing the contingencies in the environment that maintain it.

The specific example we will discuss in this section is a case history of the treatment of a severely disturbed 3½-year-old boy named Dicky. The case was published in a journal called *Behaviour Research and Therapy* by three investigators, Montrose M. Wolf, Todd R. Risley, and Hayden L. Mees (1964). These investigators systematically applied principles developed in the laboratory to Dicky's very self-destructive behavior.

Dicky appeared to be a normal child until he was nine months old, when it was discovered that he had cataracts in both eyes. At about this time he began having trouble going to sleep and also began to display unusual temper tantrums. In his second year of life he had a series of eye operations, culminating in the removal of the lenses of both eyes. This meant that in order for him to see normally, he would have to wear eyeglasses. He refused. His parents tried for a year to get him to wear glasses and to cope with his violent temper tantrums, but they could not. The authors of the article give you some idea of the severity of Dicky's behavior in the following quotation:

> Dicky did not eat normally and lacked normal social and verbal repertoires. His tantrums included self-destructive behaviors such as head-banging, face-slapping, hair-pulling, and face-scratching. His mother reported that after a severe tantrum "he was a mess, all black and blue and bleeding." He would not sleep at night, forcing one or both parents to remain by his bed. Sedatives, tranquilizers, and restraints were tried, without success (pp. 305–306).

Dicky's parents took him to a variety of specialists and got a variety of diagnoses. Finally, when he was three, they had him admitted to a mental hospital for children, where his condition was diagnosed as childhood schizophrenia. (This is an extremely serious condition which is difficult to treat effectively.) He was released in three months with the report that there had been some improvement. However, there had been no success in the effort to get Dicky to wear glasses. Dicky's ophthalmologist now told the parents that unless he began to wear glasses within six months, he would become virtually blind—permanently.

At this point, Wolf, Risley, and Mees were asked to consult in the case and to try to train Dicky to wear glasses. They began by observing a twenty-minute interaction between Dicky and his mother. They observed what was practically a twenty-minute temper tantrum. They recommended that Dicky be readmitted to the hospital so that he would be separated from his mother while they tried to reduce the undesired behavior and to train him to wear glasses.

The three psychologists themselves did not work with the child. They worked with the ward attendants and with the parents. Careful instructions were given to these people. They were told how to treat Dicky and exactly what behaviors and environmental events to record.

Detailed, accurate record-keeping is crucial for several reasons. The behavior modification approach to treatment of abnormal behavior assumes that the *consequences* of a specific behavior are a powerful determinant of whether or not that behavior will be repeated. If we are to change behavior by manipulating its consequences, that is, systematically rewarding and punishing it, we have to have detailed records of the responses, the manipulations (rewards and punishments), and other outside events which may be influencing that behavior. Otherwise, we would not know how to modify our manipulation during the course of therapy. And we would not know what specific manipulations had led to what specific behavior changes, if the therapy were successful in modifying the behavior.

Wolf, Risley, and Mees decided to deal with several aspects of Dicky's behavior concurrently. They attempted to reduce his tantrums and his sleeping and eating problems. On the positive side, they attempted to teach Dicky to keep his glasses on, not to throw them, and to establish appropriate verbal and social behavior. We will examine in detail two of these.

TEMPER TANTRUMS. If you will recall, Dicky's tantrums were violent and self-destructive. Under normal circumstances, the consequences of temper tantrums are unpredictable. Parents are often quite perplexed and threatened by this behavior, and respond to it by ignoring, punishing, or cuddling the child, depending on their mood, the particular circumstances of the tantrum, and other factors which may be unknown to the child. As a matter of fact, it is a kind of standard scene in situation television comedies:

1. Child throws tantrum
2. Mother scolds and fusses at child
3. Child continues
4. Mother threatens to tell Father
5. Father enters, Mother demands he spank child
6. Father spanks
7. Mother scolds Father
8. Mother loves and cuddles child

If the consequences of behavior are significant determinants of future behavior, what systematic effects can possibly occur if the consequences are, so far as the child can determine, so completely unpredictable?

Wolf, Risley, and Mees made sure the consequences were systematic. Every time Dicky threw a tantrum, he was placed in his room and his door was closed until the tantrum ceased. In order to collect the kinds of data needed, and also in order to communicate clearly with the ward attendants and parents, a temper tantrum was defined objectively. A tantrum was the simultaneous occurrence of two or more of the following three behaviors: whining, crying, face-slapping. A severe tantrum was defined as involving more seriously self-destructive behavior: head-banging, hair-pulling, or face-scratching. Although this mild punishment involved some rewarding aspects, in the form of social contact and individual attention, it removed the possibility of continuous attention during the tantrum and also provided for rewarding nontantrum behavior. The door was opened when the tantrum stopped, and therefore door-opening was contingent upon Dicky's performing some other behavior, any other behavior as long as it was incompatible with tantrums. As the time passed, Dicky's parents were permitted to visit him, and he began making trips home. These events, summarized below, are marked on Figure 2, (p. 72), which presents the data for severe tantrums:

> At (a) Dicky's parents were permitted their first one-hour visit. Subsequently they made several scheduled visits a week, during which an attendant observed and instructed them in their handling of Dicky.
>
> At (b) the father put Dicky to bed on the ward for the first time.
>
> At (c) Dicky began wearing his glasses.

At (d) the mother put Dicky to bed on the ward for the first time.

Midway between (d) and (e) Dicky began short home visits accompanied by the attendant.

At (e) Dicky spent his first night at home.

At (f) Dicky spent a second night at home.

After (f) he spent an average of three nights a week at home, increasing to five nights a week during the final month (p. 307).

The graph speaks volumes. Dicky's severe tantrums became progressively rarer as the behavior modification program progressed. You can judge for yourself the effects of the various events, such as home visits, from the graph. It seems that Dicky's tantrums were fairly well under the control of the systematic environmental consequences arranged by the investigators.

GLASSES-WEARING. The problem posed here for the investigators is very different in an essential respect. In stressing the importance for future behavior of the consequences of behavior, we have been stressing one of the fundamental principles of reinforcement theory. An action that is rewarded, or reinforced, will tend to be repeated. But suppose you are interested in a rather complex response, one with a very low chance of being made. If it is not made, how can you reinforce it in the hopes of increasing its frequency? Consider the present situation. Dicky has steadfastly resisted any and all attempts, by parents, doctors, and hospital personnel alike, at making him wear glasses. Consider what might happen in Dicky's case if the investigators had no alternative but to wait for the desired response to occur so that they could reinforce it. Dicky would go blind. There is an alternative, demonstrated with remarkable clarity in the various Skinnerian animal laboratories. It is referred to as *shaping,* or *successive approximations.* If a complex response is the desired one, the experimenter simply adopts the procedure of reinforcing anything which resembles that response. When this first approximation to the desired response is a reliable part of the subject's behavior, the experimenter raises his criterion for reinforcement—that is, he waits until a better response, a closer approximation to the desired one, is made before he gives reinforcement. Progressing in this way, by a skillful use of rewards, extraordinarily complex chains of behavior can be shaped.

COULD DICKY BE SHAPED TO WEAR GLASSES? One attendant was selected to do the shaping. He was instructed in the procedure and spent two or three twenty-minute sessions with the boy each day. The reward selected for use in shaping the glasses-wearing was food: Dicky was to get small bites of candy or fruit for making the right response—or, in the beginning, approximating it. But here a problem arises. In order for shaping to be successful, the reinforcement must be delivered *immediately after the desired response*, not after some other response. If Dicky is in the far corner of the room and he makes a movement toward his head with the glasses, you can't pop a piece of food into his mouth at just the right moment. If you walk over and give him candy, he might be smashing the glasses by the time you get there. So a means of immediately delivering the reinforcement must be developed. Again the animal laboratories have given us an answer, a means to get the reinforcement *in* immediately. The trick is to take some stimulus which can be delivered from a distance and present it repeatedly in a situation in which the subject will get reinforced. In Dicky's case the procedure was to have Dicky get small bites of the candy or fruit right after the attendant made a clicking noise with a toy noisemaker. After this was done for several sessions, Dicky would go to the bowl of reinforcers whenever he heard the clicks! The click meant food was there for the taking and now the click could be used to shape behavior. The click could be delivered quickly and from any part of the room—and now it had acquired reinforcing properties.

The shaping sessions then began by laying several pairs of glassless frames around Dicky's rooms. He was reinforced in the beginning just for picking them up and holding or carrying them. Then he was reinforced for bringing them close to his head, then for putting them on. Problems developed, however. The attendant-shaper could not get Dicky to put the glasses on straight. He put them on so that the ear pieces were under, rather than over, his ears, and so that the eye holes did not line up with his eyes. Dicky's progress was essentially halted.

The investigators conceived of two possible reasons. First, the attendant was inexperienced at the shaping process. Second, the ward staff was reluctant to deprive Dicky of food, and the reinforcers being used were therefore relatively weak. After two weeks, action was taken to remedy the second possibility. Dicky's breakfast was made contingent upon approximations to glasses-wearing. He would get his breakfast, a bite at a time, depending on his responses. Two more fruitless weeks passed, and the glasses themselves were modified with larger earpieces and a "roll-bar" going over the top of the head to keep the earpieces up over the ears. Another week passed without success, and the investigators themselves intervened. They spent a day with the attendant and Dicky, directing the shaping procedures. They added a second bar to the glasses, this time to the back. In effect, the glasses were now put on and worn like a cap. They began the shaping at breakfast time, with bites of food again being contingent upon approximations to glasses-wearing. The breakfast session was ineffective. So Dicky got little to eat. This time, however, lunch was used as a shaping session also. Dicky's glasses-wearing behavior did not improve, so he again did not get much to eat. A third session was carried out at about two in the afternoon, and Dicky's motivation level was high, he was very hungry. He seemed particularly interested in the ice cream which the three psychologists happened to have brought with them. It was clear that the deprivation had greatly increased the power of the reinforcers, and now the investigators elected to use the prescription lenses rather than the empty frames. There was a great deal of behavior like the right behavior, and the investigators had a relatively easy time picking out better and better approximations. At the end of thirty minutes they had reinforced both the putting on and looking through the glasses sufficiently so that they could show Dicky interesting objects, with the hope of maintaining his "looking behavior." After this, his progress was rapid, and he wore his glasses continuously while he was eating. Soon, a variety of other, less concrete reinforcers were maintaining the behavior. For example, the attendant would take Dicky for a walk if he was wearing his glasses, but the walk would be terminated if he took the glasses off. When Dicky was released from the hospital, he was wearing his glasses for an average of twelve hours a day. The results are illustrated by Figure 3.

What a difference! Just compare this study with any other one you have read so far. The previous investigators were trying to develop an understanding of behavior with the hope of later controlling it. The research tradition represented by Wolf, Risley, and Mees sees the control of behavior as an immediately attainable goal, perhaps as the only worthwhile goal. You have read what they did. You may have some ideas about why Dicky's behavior changed, perhaps in terms of expectancies, or perhaps will power. Just note that Wolf, Risley, and Mees did not theorize. They did not think it was necessary.

If we analyze the "experiment" in terms of what has been written about the other studies, we might consider it to be deficient with respect to the use of formal experimental controls. Only one boy's data were reported and no control group was used. However, Dicky acted as his own control. If

FIGURE 2.

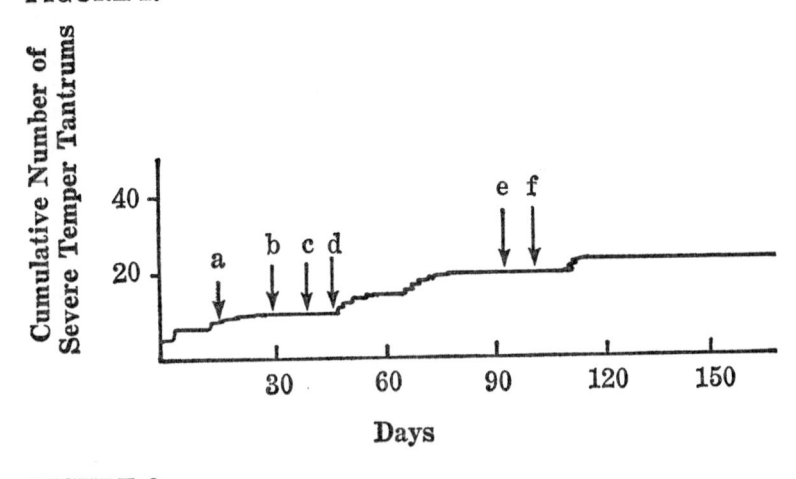

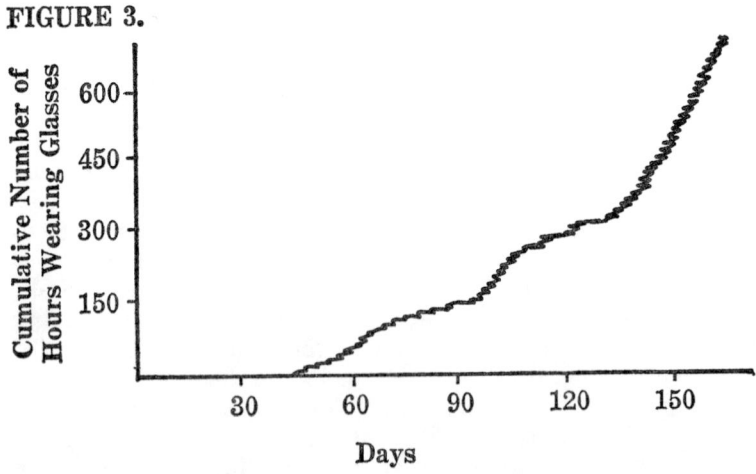

[Graph: Cumulative Number of Severe Temper Tantrums vs. Days, with arrows labeled a, b, c, d, e, f]

FIGURE 3.

[Graph: Cumulative Number of Hours Wearing Glasses vs. Days]

Figures 2 and 3 represent cumulative response curves for severe temper tantrums and glasses-wearing, respectively. These can be best understood if you think of them as being made by a marker pen which moves up one unit as the paper moves slowly under the pen. A portion of the curve which is horizontal indicates that *no responses* were made during the time covered by that portion. Thus, in Figure 2, no severe temper tantrums at all were made after about the 105th day. The slope of the cumulative curve is a direct measure of the rate of responding. The shape of the curve in Figure 3 indicates that, generally speaking, once Dicky got started wearing glasses, he wore them for longer and longer periods each day, until he leveled off at about the 150th day at a rate of 12 hours per day.

we compare his pretreatment and posttreatment behavior, there were dramatic changes. Furthermore, Dicky was being compared with a large number of control subjects. There are many, many children like him who do not get treated and who do not improve. In yet another sense, Dicky was being compared with many control subjects. The investigators were using a set of very highly controlled conditions which were developed in hundreds of laboratories on literally thousands upon thousands of subjects representing many species. These conditions—the rewards, punishments, and the stimuli which accompany them—have been studied on a multitude of controls, from mice to pigeons to children to men.

Before making our concluding remarks which bring this study back to our original question, let us consider a possible error in interpretation. The fact that Dicky's disturbed behavior can be modified through the use of learning principles does not necessarily mean that this disturbed behavior was learned. It is the case that biologically determined behaviors can be radically modified by learning. If you want a powerful example of this, just consider the effects described in the section on voodoo death. The kind of disorder Dicky had may have been biological or it may have been learned.

There are many psychologists who believe that this behavior modification approach is the most exciting thing to happen in psychotherapy in a long time, but there are many other psychologists who have grave doubts. Those who regard abnormal behavior as a *mental illness,* as a *disease entity,* regard this approach as nothing other than treating symptoms.

How does this study, then, relate to the grand question? What does it tell us? It tells us that there is a vigorous movement in psychology, a minority movement though it may be, which is answering the question by shouting back: That's the wrong question!

BRIEF DESCRIPTIONS OF OTHER STUDIES OF STRESS AND PERSONALITY

In the preceding sections we have presented nine research studies in some depth. They employed a variety of stressors, ranging from electric shock to immersion in water. The indices of personality change, the behavior changes observed, varied from answers to a questionnaire to ulceration and death. The investigators used a wide sampling of living organisms as subjects, including rats, monkeys, and men. We have deliberately selected studies which represent a variety of approaches since one of our purposes in presenting these research examples is to demonstrate the breadth and complexity of the original question posed by the student. Even though variety was one of the criteria by which we selected studies, we have really presented only a minute sampling of the literature on stress and personality change. We have described nine of the experiments which have been published in the past twenty or so years, but there are actually thousands of research studies published each and every year dealing with the effects of stress.

We would like to demonstrate further the complexity —and unanswerability—of the original, unrefined, grand question. We will try to accomplish this by relating to you, with a minimum of detail, some of the other investigations into the effects of stress. In selecting these studies to be briefly presented, we are still applying the criterion of variety. Obviously, from what has been said above, nothing even remotely approaching comprehensiveness of coverage is being attempted.

The US Navy has been conducting a major research program centering on the ability of men to live and work for long periods of time under the sea. A significant aspect of this program involves the attempt to assess the psychological impact of the multiple, unusual stresses involved in undersea life. The psychological components of this project are discussed in a fascinating book, *Groups Under Stress: Psychological Research in Sealab II* (Radloff and Helmreich, 1968). The book details the men's reactions, not only to the environmental stresses involved in living undersea and going on long diving missions outside their habitat, but also the social stresses of living together in close quarters over extended periods of time.

In *The Threat of Impending Disaster: Contributions to the Psychology of Stress* by Grosser, Wechsler, and Greenblatt, research on the environmental stresses involved in exploring *space* is discussed by Ruff and Korchin (1964), a psychiatrist and a psychologist. They have investigated not only the life history and present personality characteristics of the Mercury astronauts, but also their responses to the stresses of space flight.

R. S. Lazarus (1964) presents some laboratory research in which stress was created by showing the subjects a "threatening" film. In this research the reactions observed were psychophysiological responses such as those described in Johnson's research above. The film threatened, or *produced stress in*, the subjects by showing a very crude, very painful ritual operation on the genitals of adolescent boys in a primitive society.

The psychiatrist, R. J. Lifton (1964), presents his analysis of the long-term psychological effects of the atomic bomb blast on those who survived Hiroshima. Lifton went to Japan seventeen years after the nuclear explosion and interviewed a large number of people who had been there. Even after seventeen years, the influences of the disaster were so profound that Lifton reported that the *interviews* left *him* shocked, and emotionally spent.

The effects of a most extreme form of stress—internment in a concentration camp—is discussed by Biderman (1964), and C. B. Bahnsen (1964) explores reactions to the threat of annihilation, recalling some of his own emotional responses as he fled and hid from the Nazi Gestapo in World War II. He analyzes the written reflections of a young Danish freedom fighter who made notes between torture sessions before he was killed by the Gestapo. Bahnsen also discusses the effects that physical illnesses occurring under the threat of imminent death have on personality.

In one way or another every investigation we have presented thus far has involved the observation of some behavioral change in the organism which seemed to be a consequence of some environmental event, of some change or difference in the environment. In many of the studies the environment was deliberately manipulated by the investigator. In others, especially some of those just cited, the investigator made his observations after some environmental event *not* under his control had occurred.

A series of studies by S. B. Sarason and his colleagues takes a still different tack (Sarason, Davidson, Lighthall, Waite, and Ruebush, 1960). This research into the question of why a person's personality changes when under stress is not aimed at predicting behavior from differences in the environment, but rather it is aimed at predicting how different individuals will behave differently, given a stressful environmental event. Sarason has focused upon performance on examinations and how that performance is affected by the anxiety of the test-takers. He approached the problem by using paper-and-pencil psychological tests to measure what he called "test-anxiety." He and his colleagues developed a questionnaire specifically designed to tap this construct, and called it the Test-Anxiety Questionnaire. They demonstrated that the children who responded differently to their questionnaire did perform differently on examinations, and did react differently to anxiety-manipulating instructions. The students' performance on school tests differed as predicted by their questionnaire performance even though the students were equivalent in what are more generally considered to be the determiners of academic achievement.

A thorough description of this research would require an entire section like those presented previously in Part II, but the essential character of Sarason's work should be clear from what has been said. Sarason was not looking at behavioral differences which result from an environmental event, like shock. Rather, he was looking at differences in the behavior of different subjects in relation to the same environmental event, an examination, as a function of the subjects' *anxiety* about taking examinations, as measured by a questionnaire.

Brief descriptions of investigations on stress and personality could continue almost indefinitely. There have been thousands, for the concept has been applied widely. We have not even mentioned some entire areas of stress research, such as stresses in business organizations (see, for example, Kahn, Wolfe, Quinn, and Snoek, 1964), and military stress research (for example, Grinker and Spiegel, 1945; Basowitz, Persky, Korchin, and Grinker, 1955). There have been numerous conferences devoted to the topic of stress. A recent one (Appley and Trumbull, 1967) brought together scientists to discuss physiological, psychophysiological, emotional, cognitive, and social aspects of stress.

While we cannot even begin to name the major figures contributing to our knowledge of stress and its effects on personality, we must mention the work of Hans Selye (1956). It was Selye who brought the construct of stress into systematic usage in the behavioral sciences. It was Selye who made stress an important theoretical concept. In his medical research Selye saw clusters of relationships in environmental events and in their biological effects which had escaped the attention of other investigators. He noted that a wide variety of biological responses all had something in common, and he labeled this common core the general adaptation syndrome. He noted, too, that this syndrome could be brought about by a wide variety of hurtful environmental events, both physical and psychological. Thus, these events had effects in common, and he labeled these events *stressors*. Stress quickly became a construct of considerable interest to investigators interested in behavior. As the reader can see, it is a construct with wide ramifications, as is the construct of personality. Both can be defined and measured in a wide variety of ways. The question of the relationship between them is not one question, but many.

Part III

Conclusions

In Part I of this book we presented a list of rather broad questions asked by students on the first day of an introductory psychology class. One was selected and analyzed word by word. In the remainder of that opening section we tried to show that such questions are essentially unanswerable, in the scientific sense. In Part II we presented a few questions related to the one analyzed in Part I. These questions were answerable because the investigators had reduced them to specific operations. We tried to place into sharp focus the differences between the *answerable* questions attacked by these investigators and the unanswerable ones so often broached by nonresearchers. Furthermore, we tried to exemplify the diversity of the modes of attack, and at the same time some of the essential similarities underlying all of the diverse attacks.

In Part III we will use the research studies of Part II as reference points to make explicit some of the important ideas about the science of behavior which have been more or less implicit in everything we have written up to now. We will first discuss some specific issues, then conclude with a more general treatment of what we believe are some of the influences which will determine the shape of the questions which future investigators will be asking.

SOME PRINCIPLES OF RESEARCH

CONTROL. One of the major elements of any scientific investigation is *control*. In the present context control does not refer to one's being able to direct, or guide, or have control over events in the way that Wolf, Risley, and Mees achieved control over Dicky's temper tantrums. Rather, control refers to operations which enable us to say, after we have carried out an experiment, that it was factor A which led to the results, not factors B, C, D, or E. *All scientific investiga-*

tions include control operations. This is true even though the *nature* of these operations varies greatly from experiment to experiment.

One basic means through which control may be achieved is by the use of control groups. Control groups permit the researcher to make comparisons between the effects of the particular manipulation he is investigating and the effects of other manipulations, or between his manipulation and no manipulation at all. Another basic technique for providing such comparisons is by the use of the subject as his own control. While the operations involved are different from a control-group design, these two experimental strategies are conceptually very similar. Researchers may choose to obtain the needed control comparisons by using either of the two approaches just outlined. A third control procedure which is closely related to the two above is the general strategy of keeping all things *constant* across groups or subjects, everything except the specific manipulation that is under examination. With this brief, general background in mind let's now examine how these principles are exemplified in the research presented in Part II.

The control-group technique is illustrated by Hunt's investigation of the effects of infant feeding frustration on adult hoarding behavior. In order to evaluate his hypothesis Hunt made *comparisons* between *different* groups of rats. Recall that he compared the hoarding behavior of rats that were frustrated in infancy with rats that did not receive this treatment in early life. Recall also that in order to evaluate the "early age" part of the hypothesis, other control groups were needed, groups that provided comparisons between early and later feeding frustration with respect to hoarding behavior. If he had not used the control groups he did, he could not have drawn the inferences from the research that he drew.

Control groups were used in a very similar manner by Masserman in his efforts to determine the role of conflict in the development of experimental neuroses, by Johnson in his study of physiological arousal, and by Schachter in his work on affiliation.

While many researchers use groups of subjects to attain control, the specific way in which these groups are used varies greatly. The variations are dependent upon both the nature of the question being asked and the factor to be controlled. Consider Brady's work on ulceration. His control group was made up of a number of monkeys which were yoked individually to an experimental, or "executive," monkey. Brady thus had the comparison he needed to evaluate his data. He could make postmortem comparisons between the stomachs of animals who were required to respond in order to avoid shock and those who were not. Brady's study also provides a good example of the general control strategy of keeping constant all possible sources of change other than the one under study. Each yoked control animal experienced *everything* that his experimental partner did except that he could not avoid shock.

When compared to their experimental partners, the yoked controls experienced equal shock, equal time in a restraining chair, equal lighting in the experimental room, and so forth. The only thing different was that the control subjects could not respond in order to avoid shock. The executive monkeys could. Possible sources of change were also held constant at another level which is probably obvious to the reader. The animals were all Rhesus monkeys. Therefore, possible phylogenetic differences were eliminated. Along the same lines, the use of animals ensured that there were no significant differences in the subjects' past history which could have accounted for ulceration, when it occurred. In fact there is a more general point to be made here. One reason for using animals as subjects is that we usually know or can control their past history. Many research questions require that we have very specific knowledge of our subject's developmental and psychological past.

We don't want to create the impression that Brady was the only researcher included in Part II who applied control in the sense of keeping things constant. If the reader will review any study presented he will discover that in some way they all utilized this fundamental principle of scientific research.

In addition to experiments in which specific groups are used to achieve control, many researchers employ the "subject-as-his-own-control" design. When control groups are used, the essential question is: How does the behavior of the control group differ from the behavior of the experimental group? For example, do rats frustrated in infancy hoard more than nonfrustrated ones? Often it is more convenient, more efficient, or more appropriate to use subjects as their own controls. When a research question is attacked by this type of design, the question might be phrased: Does a subject's (or group of subjects') behavior *change* as a function of a specific, experimental manipulation? In this type of experimental design the researcher observes some selected aspect of behavior of his subjects at a given point in time. He then carries out his experimental manipulation on these subjects and again observes their behavior. No separate control groups are used, for the subjects are literally their own control groups. Many questions can be approached with either design.

Miller's research on stress and learning provides an example of the subjects-as-their-own-control design. Recall that in order to test his hypothesis Miller chose to carry his experiment out in a series of steps or stages. His first step was to demonstrate that the white compartment was a neutral stimulus. The final step demonstrated that rats would learn a novel response, wheel turning, to escape this previously neutral compartment. The important point for our purposes is that all of the steps were carried out with the *same* rats. Step one provided control comparisons for step two, and so forth. This will be very clear if the reader will refer back to the section on stress and learning (beginning on page 31) and look at the comparisons made as Miller's research progressed from step to step.

Wolf, Risley, and Mees' work with Dicky provides another example of a subject used as his own control. Before the treatment procedures were implemented the boy had temper tantrums and refused to wear his glasses. It was possible to demonstrate systematic changes in Dicky's behavior as the work progressed.

Early in this section we reiterated the argument that before research can be considered scientific it is necessary that controls be applied. Can we argue that Cannon's study of "voodoo" death is scientific, given this criterion? Remember that the purpose of using controls is to rule out alternative explanations of the findings. Cannon did attempt this. Through a careful review of the literature he tried to rule out deaths due to old age, poison, disease, and so forth. While the nature of the question made it impossible for him to apply experimental controls, he did use the *concept* of control in seeking out data which would allow him to rule out other possible interpretations of the phenomenon.

There are many, many control techniques which we have not focused on here. In order to insure comparability of groups so that differences can be attributed to the experimental manipulation, researchers can randomly assign subjects to groups, or they can make up matched groups. The latter is accomplished by carefully selecting and assigning subjects to groups on the basis of some dimension relevant to the study. In some experiments it is necessary to control for effects like practice over time. A technique known as counterbalancing is used in situations such as this.

It is not our purpose to outline or explain all of the possible approaches that one may take to obtain control. Rather it is our purpose to make abundantly clear the importance of control in scientific research. While control has many guises, the fundamental purpose is the same.

Without adequate controls we cannot meaningfully interpret research data. Without adequate controls we cannot meaningfully answer our research questions.

There is an important point that we must raise here. No matter how well controlled a particular study is, an investigator can never be sure that he has ruled out *every* possible event which could have produced his results. In fact, researchers don't try to study *all* of the possible events relating to any one aspect of behavior. For example, Masserman could not state that experimental neurosis is caused *only* by conflict. Perhaps sensory deprivation could also lead to neurotic behavior, perhaps the stress of having to make "executive decisions" could produce neurotic behavior. Masserman could not say, for he did not study these antecedents as they relate to experimental neurosis. He *did* rule out events like experiencing an air blast or feeding frustration in the absence of conflict. He was able to say that these events which were *inherent* in his research did not, in and of themselves, produce experimental neurosis.

Hunt provides another example of the same point. As we have seen, he applied controls appropriate to asking the question: Does feeding frustration in infancy lead to adult hoarding behavior? But he *cannot* say that experiencing electric shock in infancy does not lead to adult hoarding behavior. It may. But this latter question is irrelevant to Hunt's research. If he wanted to rule out shock as an important antecedent condition he would have had to include in his study another control group—a group that experienced shock.

Thus, while we have repeatedly written throughout this volume that the purpose of control is to rule out alternative explanations of the results of an experiment, this statement is actually true in only a limited sense. The only alternative explanations ruled out by good experimental control are those which are possible, direct consequences of manipulations used in carrying out the research. Masserman's controls did not rule out sensory deprivation as a possible antecedent condition of experimental neurosis. He could not and did not control for *all possible* sources of influence on a particular aspect of behavior. This is a criticism of neither Masserman nor Hunt. These comments apply generally to psychological research. No piece of research is a complete specification of all antecedent conditions leading to a particular behavioral change.

There is an important point implicit in the above discussion. The basic assumption which an experimenter makes about behavior in general, and about the behavior under investigation in particular, determines the experimental manipulations and the control operations he will employ. These assumptions, at the same time that they enable him to make sense out of some small aspect of behavior, drastically *limit* what he can observe. An investigator cannot obtain information about the potential influence of a condition that he has controlled precisely because he has elected to control that influence. Similarly, he cannot obtain information about the potential effect of any number of other conditions that are simply not included in the research. The possible outcomes of a research project are considerably constrained by the initial beliefs, assumptions, and biases of the investigator.

RESEARCH STRATEGIES. As has been amply demonstrated in Part II of this book, there are many different ways of investigating answerable questions. The research methodologies ranged from creating whole, artificial environments in which stimulation was reduced to a minimum, to reading the account of strange deaths that had been reported by other investigators.

The apparatus utilized by the investigators included boxes with grid floors and black and white walls (Miller), phony shock apparatus (Schachter), special restraining chairs (Brady), test booklets (Sarason), and a half-gallon of ice cream (Wolf, Risley, and Mees)! Other investigators utilized no apparatus as such; they explored the effects of stress on personality by going into life situations where great stresses were known to have occurred, as in the study on the long-term effects of the atomic bombing of Hiroshima.

Similarly, the subjects in the few studies presented varied considerably. The subject populations from which the samples were selected included rats, monkeys, college sophomores, and psychiatrists.

All of the above emphasizes the heterogeneity, the differences, in research strategies. Are there any major similarities which run through all of the studies cited, and through all of the investigations which bear the name *scientific?* The answer is clearly yes! One of the major similarities is the requirement that at some point in the research process we get to the level of observation. Given this major commonality across research studies, are there any fundamental distinctions among types of research? That is, can we categorize research along any dimensions more fundamental than the subjects used, the apparatus employed, and the content area involved? Again, the answer is yes! We will focus on one of the major distinctions, that between *manipulative* and *nonmanipulative* research. This is an extremely significant categorization when discussing research in psychology. The distinction often goes under the name of experimental (manipulative) versus nonexperimental research. Actually, almost every section in Part II except the last one was devoted to rather complete expositions of research in which the experimenter manipulated the subjects' environment in some way. Hunt deprived his rats of food. Brady electrically shocked his monkeys. Schachter threatened his student subjects with shock. Miller shocked his rats in a specially constructed environment. Shurley created an entirely artificial environment for his subjects, immersing them in a tank of water. Masserman deprived his cats of food and stimulated them with electric shocks and air blasts. Johnson, too, stimulated his students with electric shocks. Finally, Wolf, Risley, and Mees manipulated Dicky's environment by making the delivery of food contingent upon certain, specific behaviors. They also went to the trouble of instructing everybody around Dicky just how to respond to him when he behaved in certain ways.

What all of the above investigators did was to select a particular aspect of the subjects' environment and *manipulate* it systematically. They then observed the subjects' behavior—or rather they observed those aspects of the subjects' behavior in which they were interested. This is the standard outline for *experimental*, or manipulative, research, and we would like to emphasize its importance by summarizing it below:

1. Vary an aspect of the environment.
2. Hold other aspects of the environment constant.
3. Observe any variations in the subjects' behavior.
4. See if the variations in the subjects' behavior are associated with variations in the subjects' environment.

Experimental research is indeed a powerful tool in the hands of an imaginative scientist. But it is not the only method. There are a variety of other methods which scientists use, several of which were presented in the closing section of Part II. One of the major forms of nonmanipulative research is called *correlational research*. It involves careful observation and measurement of two or more different aspects of the subjects' behavior, and then determining whether or not these different aspects are related in any systematic way. If correlational research does lead to statements of lawful relationships between two aspects of behavior, then it enables the investigator to make *predictions* about behavior. That is, he can predict, with some accuracy, one aspect of behavior from his knowledge of another aspect of behavior. For example, if there is a known, lawful relationship between grades in mathematics courses and grades in physics courses, then one could predict someone's physics grade by knowing his math grade. The prediction would not be perfect, but it would be better than a prediction made on the basis of no information. This kind of knowledge, knowledge about the relationship between behaviors, can be extraordinarily valuable in situations where one of the behaviors is easy to observe and measure, and the other is extremely difficult, or very costly, to get at. We would like to present a fairly lengthy, actual example of correlational research in just such a situation. It involves the development of a paper-and-pencil test to predict success in pilot-training school. A paper-and-pencil test is very cheap and easy to give. With the large group on which the Air Force developed the test, it was found by correlational research that the test predicted remarkably well which members of the group would ultimately "wash out" of pilot-training school. In this case prediction means that if someone attains a high score on the test, he will very likely succeed in training, while an individual who gets a low score is likely to fail. In this original group on which the correlational research was done, *everyone* was tested and *everyone* went on to pilot-training school. But the practical use of the test came with later groups. Since the test predicted success and failure well in the original group, it was assumed that the test would predict success and failure of subsequent applicants as well. This was true since the characteristics of the applicants did not change in any systematic fashion and since the training program stayed the same. Given these assumptions, the test results could be used as one important source of information in deciding whether or not to accept an applicant or reject him. Thus, in the thousands of cases after the test was developed, the inexpensive, easy-to-get test score could be used in the selection of applicants, and a much, much smaller proportion washed out. Not only is the training school spared the very large expense involved in partially training someone only to see him fail to complete the program, but many individuals are spared the major disappointment involved in failing. Errors are certainly made. Some applicants who are selected do not make it. Some who are rejected would have made it had they been accepted. But their numbers are fewer than would have been the case had the test not been developed and used.

    Examples of correlational research abound in the psychological literature. Sarason's (1960) work relating anxiety as measured by the Test-Anxiety Questionnaire to performance on examinations in school is another example of this form of research. Prediction of college grades, imperfect though such prediction may be, from college-board scores, is somewhat successful because of a great deal of research which *correlated* the *predictor* and the *predicted* behaviors. Prediction of school success from IQ tests also rests upon many years of such correlational research. In all of these instances, which exemplify essentially practical applications, a very hard-to-get segment of behavior is predicted by a much more accessible segment, test scores.

There are many examples of correlational research which involve questions of almost purely theoretical interest rather than questions related to application. For an example somewhat more closely related to the question that has been the theme of this book, a psychologist by the name of R. R. Sears (1961) has investigated the relationship between punitiveness of mothers and aggressiveness of their children. The measures of both of these constructs, punitiveness and aggression, involved ratings by individuals who could observe *behaviors* which would be counted as punitive or as aggressive. Other investigators have used the correlational method to determine whether or not two aspects of personality are typically associated with one another in the same individuals, for instance, conformity and anxiety, or general intelligence and dominance of others.

Experimental and correlational research are the two major forms of research distinguished by most psychologists. Some who write about the topic regard all nonexperimental, nonmanipulative research as correlational. Others restrict the meaning of correlational research more, and have classification schemes including other forms of research, such as the case history method and the survey method. For our purposes though, a crucial distinction hinges on whether or not the investigator manipulates the subject's environment in some way.

We chose to present predominantly manipulative research in Part II for several reasons. First, the nature of the grand question, How does personality change under stress? is such that it lends itself nicely to manipulative research. Secondly, the selection of a few studies from thousands of possibilities reflects the authors' biases. It is our belief, and the belief of many, many psychologists, that whenever a research question can be attacked experimentally, the experimental approach is preferable to other possible alternatives. The reason is fairly straightforward and can be found in the section immediately preceding this one. The reason can be expressed in one word, *control.* While all scientific methods involve control, the experimental method allows for the greatest degree of control. In the experimental method the antecedent condition of interest is being manipulated. At the same time other antecedent conditions which may potentially affect the consequent behavior of interest, but with which the investigator is not concerned at the moment, may be controlled right out of the experiment. Because of this characteristic, the experimentally oriented investigator can often isolate precisely which antecedent condition is influencing the behavior of the subjects. Thus, it is experimental research which will yield cause-effect relationships. This is not true of correlational research, the case history method, the survey method, or any other method which involves only observation and measurement. Let us take just one of the nonmanipulative studies as an illustration of these points. When Lifton interviewed the atomic bomb survivors, he found lingering effects after a seventeen-year span. The question may be raised: Effects of what? Lifton himself pointed out that the survivors were given a special name by their neighbors and were regarded as in some ways inferior. Changes had no doubt taken place. But were they due to the massive shock experienced at the moment of impact or to seeing the unparalleled suffering in the aftermath of the bomb? Or, perhaps even to radiation-induced biological differences? Or, as implied above, perhaps the effects were due to the long-term discrimination against the victims by those unaffected by the bomb. There is simply no way of knowing.

This statement about the inability of nonmanipulative research to yield cause-effect relationships is by no means a devaluing of these methodologies. If the reader will reflect upon the examples of nonmanipulative research, it will become evident that there are a wide variety of interesting, important, and answerable questions which are simply not amenable to experimental manipulation. In fact, there are entire fields of science, astronomy for one, which do not employ any sort of manipulative methodology. In psychology one of the many classes of questions which must be approached correlationally is the development of psychological tests. How could an investigator employ manipulative research in attacking the problem of predicting who will be successful in pilot training? What is needed for that prediction is some measure of the performance of the applicant from which pilot training performance can be predicted. This is essentially the definition of correlational research—the prediction of one kind of performance from another, the prediction of one kind of behavior from another. If you will consider the other research questions advanced above in the illustrations of nonmanipulative research, you will see that they simply cannot be approached by the experimental method. How can one study the influence of atomic bomb blasts on personality experimentally? One cannot.

There are different research strategies available. Which one the investigator selects is at least partly determined by the research question he is asking.

REPLICATION. The necessity of carrying out *repeatable, controlled* observations has been strongly emphasized. As we have already discussed the concept of control and its implications for research, we now wish to focus briefly upon the other important concept, repeatability.

We have already seen that it is necessary for a researcher to carry out his work in a manner that will allow others to make the same observations. But why is this necessary? If research is carried out well, don't the findings represent scientific facts? Not necessarily. There are many reasons why it is important to repeat, or to replicate, already completed work. Let's discuss a few of them.

No matter how carefully one carries out a piece of research, the question must be raised: How reliable are the findings? That is, before accepting a discovered relationship as a fact and before attempting to extend the work or to integrate the findings with other data, we should be certain that the effects are "real," that they are not produced by some unique characteristic or combination of characteristics of the subjects, the laboratory, the apparatus, and so forth. Ideally, the way to insure this is to carry out the research again, with precisely the same methodology. If the findings are the same, that is, if the research is replicable, then we are more confident of the effects. If not, it is necessary to examine the methods even more carefully and to attempt to determine why the previous findings were not replicated. This may lead to further questioning and research and perhaps an even greater understanding of the phenomena under examination. Or it may leave important questions still unanswered and demand further research. For example, a few years ago Wolpe (1966), a research-oriented psychiatrist, attempted to replicate Masserman's work on experimental neurosis. He found something that Masserman's careful work had apparently ruled out. Wolpe reports that his subjects developed experimental neurosis without conflict being present in the situation. The only step open now is for researchers to study this particular problem in even greater detail in order to resolve the apparent contradiction.

But attempting to demonstrate the reliability of our findings is only part of the story. It is also important to demonstrate things like the generality of our effects. For example, we may find a particular relationship or effect to be a very reliable one when college students are used as subjects. If we wish to make fairly general statements about our findings, that is, be certain that the effects hold for adults outside the college population, a replication may be necessary. In this case the research would be carried out in *exactly* the same way as before with the only exception being the differences in subjects.

In actual practice we often combine our efforts to replicate previous work with extensions of that work. Our experiment may include in it a previous piece of research, perhaps represented by two or three groups, while the remaining groups of subjects are treated in a different way to provide additional information. For instance, one of the present authors collaborated on research concerning the relationship between the stress due to escapable versus inescapable shock and loss of body weight (Ragusa, Shemberg, and Rasbury, 1968). It was found that rats who could push a bar to *escape* a shock lost less weight than rats exposed to the same pattern, duration, and intensity of inescapable shocks. For a variety of reasons it may be judged important to replicate these findings —that is, to demonstrate the reliability of the effect. It may also be important to determine if this relationship holds under an even more aversive level of shock. Thus, a replication might not only include groups of rats treated just as before, but also two additional groups. These would again be one group that can escape shock and one that can't, but with a higher level of shock than that previously used. In this way it would be possible to combine a check on the reliability of previous work with an extension of our knowledge of the effects of escapable versus inescapable shock on weight loss.

Many researchers carry out replications and replications with extensions of their own and others' work. It is true, however, that the science of psychology suffers to some extent from a lack of replication of some of our major research findings. There is reason, however, why researchers do not often actually do their experiments over again. This reason has to do with the mathematical procedures used in the analysis of research findings. We will deal briefly with these procedures in the following section.

QUANTIFICATION. The first time we raised the issue of quantification was in Part I, when the word *change* was being discussed. The point made there was simply that change is actually specified much more precisely when it is expressed quantitatively rather than qualitatively. We also mentioned that the issue of quantification could have been raised even earlier, in discussing the means by which terms are defined or in the discussion of measurement. It may be clear now that definition, measurement, and the specification of change are all intimately bound up with one another. The operations by which terms are defined are very often measurement operations, and most often change is reported as a difference between measurements. The change in Dicky's behavior, for example, was expressed in terms of the difference between the number of tantrums he was having in a given period of time at the end of treatment and the number he had had at the beginning.

So quantification enters the scientific picture right at the very outset. Big questions must be reduced to answerable ones by relating the terms of the question to observables—and it is a fact that *most* scientists have a very strong preference for using quantitative definitions whenever possible. If the reader will mull over the studies presented, it will become evident that this aspect of quantification has been implicitly presented time and time again throughout these pages.

Consider the following illustrations of this point, drawn from the studies reviewed. Hunt defined *young* in quantitative terms, number of days since weaning, and he defined *hoarding* quantitatively as well, in terms of the number of pellets.

Brady reported shock level in quantitative terms, and *counted* the number of experimental monkeys who ulcerated as opposed to the number of yoked controls. At this point it may be well to note that Brady had alternatives available other than counting. He could have measured the extent of the ulceration and calculated average amount of ulceration, or used some other measurement technique more elaborate than he did. He chose simply to count ulcerated monkeys in light of his experimental goals, and in light of a wide variety of factors which an investigator takes into consideration when making decisions about any part of the experiment.

Schachter, in the portions of his research which we reported above, did not attempt to quantify his manipulation of the environment. He gave the co-eds two different sets of instructions and reported a verbatim transcription of these instructions in his book. He did, however, present a quantitative statement of his measure of behavior. While he simply asked the girls if they would rather wait alone or wait with someone else, he evaluated his hypothesis by the difference in *numbers* who said they would rather be alone in the various conditions.

Johnson carefully specified his conflict manipulations in quantitative terms, detailing the number of metronome beats per second. He also defined *arousal* in a quantitative fashion, measuring and reporting heart rate, skin conductance, and palmar sweat.

Miller, too, and Wolf, Risley, and Mees employed quantification as an integral, crucial part of their research designs. The practice of selecting particular antecedent conditions and consequent behaviors such that their observation may be made and reported quantitatively rather than qualitatively permits great precision and repeatability of the observations.

Obviously, not all investigators, nor even all of those we have mentioned, are interested in problems which are easily reducible to quantifiable terms. Shurley, for example, expressed neither his manipulation nor his measure of behavior in quantitative terms. He presented a careful verbal description of the tank and associated apparatus, and gave some verbatim accounts of the subjects' verbal productions during immersion. Masserman also presented qualitative descriptions as his primary data, but he also presents some frequency counts as supporting evidence.

The reader may have noted that we have been subsuming under the labels *quantification* and *measurement* some rather different methods for assigning numbers to the phenomena of interest. In some of the cases events either occurred or did not occur, and were counted. As far as Brady was concerned, monkeys either ulcerated or they did not.

Conversely, Hunt was concerned with *how many* pellets each rat hoarded, not *whether or not* the rat hoarded. They all hoarded to some extent, but knowing how much each one hoarded enabled Hunt to assess the effects of infant feeding frustration. All of Johnson's subjects had measurable skin conductances, but the values of the measures differed drastically from person to person and from group to group. Therefore, he had to measure the degree, not the presence or absence, of skin conduction, etc. There are, in fact, several different categories of measurement. Just how much one can do with the numbers depends in part on the type of measurement used, but to discuss these here would be too much of a digression. The point is that *many* investigators strive mightily to define their manipulation and their measures of behavior in such a fashion that numerical values can be used to represent them.

There is another way in which quantification is crucial in behavioral research, the use of statistical analysis to assess the reliability of the research results. Almost always we are dealing with some small portion, or sample, of the population to which we wish to generalize. Schachter used as subjects only a very limited number of college co-eds, but he was interested in making statements about *people,* not just the college co-eds with whom he conducted his investigation. The usual way of saying this is that the investigator wishes to make generalizations from samples to the populations from which the sample is drawn. When used in this way the term *population* means every person about whom the investigator wishes to make a statement. *Sample* refers to the individuals in the population on whom observations were actually made. A simple example is that of TV ratings. The rating organization asks only a relatively few people what program they are watching—but their inferences are in terms of millions of viewers.

Now it is a fact of nature that individuals within a

population are different from one another. If an investigator does a piece of research in which he has a group whose environment he manipulates and another group which he uses as a control, he must first select the subjects in such a fashion that any prejudgments he has about the outcome cannot influence the assignment of subjects to groups. The essential procedure for ruling out the possibility of such a bias in the assignment of subjects is *random sampling* and *random assignment*. That is, subjects for experiments should be selected and assigned by chance. But the fact of individual differences remains. There is always the possibility that *the two groups will differ with respect to what is being investigated, even if no differential treatment is given.* In fact, it is very unlikely that the groups will be exactly the same. If a class of students were split into two groups by tossing a coin, it is highly probable that the average intelligence quotient of the two groups would differ at least slightly. The degree to which they would differ would depend in part upon the range of IQs in the class. If there were wide differences in IQs, there might be a wide difference between the groups. If everyone in the class had the same IQ, of course there could not be any difference between the group means. If we were to repeat the process over and over, split the class randomly into two groups and calculate the average IQs, we would find that the difference would not always be the same. This is because the degree to which the groups differ is dependent upon another factor, the laws of chance.

One of the most important consequences of using quantification in any research investigation is that the investigator can use the techniques of statistical inference to determine whether the difference he gets is due to his manipulation, or is really no larger than one would ordinarily expect due to chance fluctuation in the sampling. If the observed difference between groups is so large that it would result from chance very rarely, then it is more reasonable to ascribe it to the manipulation rather than to chance. Such differences are called "statistically significant," and this expression means only that the difference is larger than would be expected by chance alone. In this usage the term *significant* does not imply important, or socially significant.

This discussion has been couched in terms of experimental research, but the same considerations apply, with appropriate modifications, to correlational research, survey research, naturalistic observation, and so forth. Any research results which can be expressed quantitatively can be treated statistically. Any attempt to discuss the reasoning underlying the testing of research results would take us too far afield. It is sufficient at this point to understand that there are methods which enable an investigator to determine statistically how reliable his results are. Quantification allows the investigator to use these methods and thereby assess his results, and this alone is a powerful reason for the use of quantification. When an investigator uses a number of subjects rather than one (a prerequisite for statistical testing) he is in a restricted sense performing a *replication* of his research on each subject. We have already seen that important scientific results ideally have reliability checks made on them by independent investigators doing the research over, that is *replicating* the research. But as said above, another less ideal but still highly desirable method of establishing the reliability of results is by statistically assessing the results of a single experiment performed on many subjects.

Quantification plays another major role in science, one for which we have not provided an illustration in the studies cited. This role is at the theoretical level and involves mathematical descriptions of the relationships among the major constructs of a science. The really powerful examples of quantification as a theoretical tool must be borrowed from other sciences. Perhaps the most impressive well-known examples are from the fields of astronomy and physics. Think for a while about the astonishing theoretical feats accomplished with the aid of mathematics in the field of astronomy. Multitudes of observations over the centuries have been made on the motions of the planets, the moon, and the stars. We now know that the distances and speeds involved are so great that the term *astronomical* has come into general use as representing numbers which are almost inconceivably large. And yet the astronomers, in developing a theory of how the universe functions, have written complex equations describing the orbits of celestial bodies so accurately that rockets can be sent off from the earth which will land on the moon or on a planet. This requires aiming the rocket at a location in space which the target will not even be close to for months. Multitudes of observations by astronomers have been neatly organized by the mathematical equations. As the reader may know, not only did the astronomer's equations nicely organize existing knowledge about astronomic phenomena, but also enabled astronomers to predict the existence of the previously unobserved planets, Neptune and Pluto.

Psychologists, too, are attempting to express their theories in a quantitative fashion, but nothing they have yet produced matches these elegant descriptions of astronomical phenomena. What mathematical theories or models there are in psychology are intended to describe only very limited aspects of behavior. For example, there are relatively precise and well-established mathematical expressions in the areas of sensation, decision making, and simple learning.

The quantitative expression of scientific questions, theories, and hypotheses has many advantages which recall the advantages of quantitative definitions. If a theory is expressed quantitatively, it can be tested precisely. Conversely, theories that are stated only in verbal terms all too often admit to widely divergent interpretations. To the extent that this is the case, such theories cannot be tested.

So quantification enters into science at every stage of the game. It plays an essential role in the definition of the terms used in asking questions about nature, in the gathering and analysis of the evidence, and in our theorizing as well.

WHERE DO QUESTIONS COME FROM? We have focused throughout upon how researchers go about the business of answering questions. However, we have not addressed ourselves directly to the issue of where questions come from. This is a very important point to deal with as it is central to the creative process in any scientific discipline. There are, in fact, innumerable sources from which questions are derived. Let's outline a few of them and where possible point to examples in Part II of this text as illustrations.

One of the major sources giving rise to questions are our theories about behavior. We will soon discuss the nature of theory and will see that one of the basic requirements of any theoretical system is that it be stated in such a way that its propositions can be tested. Thus, many of our questions are derived directly from stated theory, and they represent attempts to substantiate the theoretical ideas. Sometimes theoretically derived questions are aimed at getting information which will enable scientists to choose between competing theories. That is, are the data consistent with theory A, or are they more consistent with theory B, a competing conceptual framework? Hunt's research is an example of a question derived from a theory. Ideally, research like this is intimately tied to the constant development and modification of our theories of behavior.

A second common source from which questions arise is the research process itself. Many researchers believe that one criterion for a good study is the number of new questions it raises. It is most often the case that an experimenter carries out a piece of research to answer a specific question. He may get his answer, but more often than not his results suggest to him a host of other questions, which may or may not be related to the original question. Perhaps while observing the behavior of his subjects a source of change that he had not even considered will occur to him. Or perhaps his results will be so different from what he has expected that they cannot be understood without further questions being answered by research. We have already seen that failure to replicate previous research requires further experimentation if the conflicting results are to be understood. Thus, the data from any one experiment can be the stimulus for a program or even a lifetime of research for the investigator.

There are times when a researcher approaches a particular question but discovers that he cannot construct an experiment to answer it. Very often this is because no one has developed a methodological technique or a particular measurement procedure that is needed for the research. These situations give rise to many questions which, in and of themselves, require research to answer. Thus, it is not unusual to find psychologists doing large-scale studies simply to answer questions about techniques which they then apply to their original research question.

In addition to the above, much research is carried out in an effort to answer real-life practical questions. Questions like, How can we select the best of a large number of applicants for a job? often lead psychologists to carry out massive research programs to construct appropriate psychological tests. Recall the development of a test for success in pilot training. Psychologists also carry out a great deal of research stimulated by practical clinical problems. For example, we try to construct tests that will tell us if a mental patient is a suicide risk. We investigate psychotherapy techniques to determine the best way to treat certain types of emotional disorders. These kinds of questions are often approached with a minimum if any interest in theoretical considerations. Rather, there is a problem "out there" which demands an answer. The question really comes from practical concerns of people in the community who are trying to get an answer to immediate, real-life questions. Wolf, Risley, and Mees' work with Dicky exemplifies to some extent this kind of an approach. The research on sensory deprivation previously described also illustrates the research approach to a practical, socially significant problem.

The sources of questions so far discussed are related either to practical problems or to already existing theory and research. However, many questions are derived from much less logical sources. Let's consider some of these.

Many times a psychologist who has been reading the results of other peoples' research says to himself, These findings are interesting. I wonder what would happen if . . . The "if" means, if I did an experiment investigating some previously unexplored relationships. Chances are the idea has not come from any serious consideration of theory. It may, in fact, come from a hunch. Schachter's work on affiliation is an example of a research project stimulated by a hunch or by intuitive reasons. This is not to say the ideas, once formalized, are less well thought through or less well developed. It is to say, however, that questions often result when an enlightened researcher sits around and thinks or argues with colleagues or talks to students.

Another source from which questions arise is just plain curiosity about the events occurring around us. Or perhaps the main source of a question is the basic excitement inherent in making sense out of something that others have not been able to explain. There are clearly many human behaviors that are just plain interesting but not understood. A researcher may simply begin with the question, I wonder what that's all about? or the statement, That doesn't make sense to me. Perhaps this is the very process that Cannon went through before he undertook his research on voodoo death.

The concept of luck is not a very scientific notion although everyone recognizes that sometimes fortuitous events may even shape history. So it is with science. Many times what turn out to be important scientific questions result from totally unexpected sources. Recall Brady's ulcer research. He and his colleagues were not looking for ulcers in their monkeys. They didn't expect them to die. But one did and he had an ulcer. This unexpected happening stimulated Brady and his colleagues to begin a whole new research program. Questions about ulcer formation and shock avoidance immediately presented themselves, and since then a number of experiments in the area have been carried out by various investigators. Similarly, B. F. Skinner reports that early in his career an apparatus failure produced interesting systematic results relating the effects of the failure to reward rats for making already learned responses.

We have discussed several sources from which scientific questions arise. There are certainly many more. The reader should recognize that the various sources outlined above are not really as independent as has been implied. For example, good hunches come in part from a solid understanding of the content of psychology and the methods of science. Also, questions arising from previous work often include theoretical interpretations. And, of course, underlying all of this is the curiosity of the scientist, the part of him that gets excited about seeking answers. Many times it is difficult to specify exactly the source of any one question, and we have not attempted to categorize each of the examples in Part II. The main point of the present section is: *Questions can come from anywhere.* There are no rules and no restrictions regarding where the scientist gets his ideas. The only rules that must be observed relate to *how the question is asked and answered.*

ETHICS. If we consider ethics to be directives or rules regarding how people should behave in order to be "good" people, or rules which tell people "right" from "wrong," then science has little to tell us about ethics. Scientific investigations provide data about the way the world *is,* but they do not answer questions about the moral or ethical goodness of that state of the world. To put it more concretely, the social scientist may be able to provide data regarding how many people *do* believe in a superior, supernatural being, but he cannot tell us if this belief is morally good or bad.

The fact that science cannot provide such answers does not mean that a scientific discipline ignores rules of ethical practice. Quite the contrary, psychology, like most professions, has a comprehensive system of rules regarding how psychologists should behave in their professional lives (American Psychological Association, 1967). In general the purpose of these rules or guidelines is to protect the public.

Given this brief general background we can now examine how psychologists apply ethical principles. We have seen that many psychologists use animals as research subjects. Certainly there are many reasons for this. As we have often pointed out above, methodological considerations and convenience represent powerful arguments for using animals as subjects. In many cases, though, ethical considerations demand the use of infrahuman subjects. Consider Brady's work on ulcer formation. The major index of stress-induced change was actual tissue damage to the organism. Brady was *trying* to produce physiological damage in an effort to understand more clearly ulcer formation in man. In fact, he stressed the animals so severely that he caused not only ulceration but death. Operations having such drastic outcomes cannot be carried out on human subjects. This is not to say that we cannot investigate ulcers in man. Certainly we can. It is possible to study ulcer patients in a wide variety of ways. We can give them psychological and physiological tests to determine how they differ from people who don't suffer from ulcers. We can study the families or social backgrounds of ulcer patients to see if these differ from those of nonulcerated persons. What we cannot do is place healthy or nonulcerated individuals in stress situations aimed at *producing* ulcers. If we want to study ulcers in humans we must wait for the events to occur. If we wish to investigate the immediate conditions leading to ulcers, the only way to do it is to manipulate the conditions we think lead to ulceration and observe the outcome. In this case the only ethical choice is to use animals as subjects. Many of the studies presented in Part II of this text were aimed at answering questions which could be ethically answered only with animal subjects. Hunt's work on feeding frustration and Masserman's research on experimental neurosis are additional examples.

The discussion so far may have led the reader to wonder if in our effort to answer questions about human behavior we are at all concerned with the humane treatment of animals. The answer is yes. There are ethical standards governing the care and treatment of research animals. These standards require proper physical care of animal subjects. It is not considered unethical to sacrifice animals, but it is unethical to do so in a way which causes them to suffer unduly. When our animals undergo pain or must be sacrificed, it is because this is the only way the information may be obtained. It is permissible only when we have some real chance of discovering something meaningful. For example, Masserman produced some rather severe behavior disorders in his cats. He was attempting to understand the conditions leading to the suffering involved in human neurosis. The expectation that he might answer significant questions concerning these conditions would have been reason enough to carry out his research. But he went even further. He provided "therapy" for the animals, not because he wanted to make them "well" but because he hoped he could shed some light on how to make people "well."

Ethical considerations are also relevant to studies involving human subjects, even though operations which might lead to lasting damage must never be used. For example, when painful stimuli are to be used, subjects are told this and not required to participate. When Johnson studied psychophysiological responses to stress, he used only volunteers who experienced a sample shock before they agreed to participate. Ethical strictures not only rule out any procedures which may lead to permanent harm, they also make it incumbent upon researchers to make certain that any negative effects at all are promptly eliminated. Consider Johnson's research again. In the case of both the difficult and the impossible discrimination groups the last few trials were made easy for the subjects. Thus they got them right, avoided shock, and likely left the experiment considerably less upset.

Another common procedure is *debriefing*. This entails informing the subjects what the experiment was all about and is particularly important whenever subjects are deliberately deceived. Think back to Schachter's studies of affiliation. In order to induce anxiety he told some subjects they would receive painful shocks. But they did not receive any shock. Schachter had to explain to them why they had been deceived and what the real purpose of the experiment was. Psychologists do not deceive subjects without carefully considering alternative methods of answering the question. If the researcher can perform a relevant experiment without deception, he does. If he cannot, he must decide if the question he is answering is important enough to warrant the operations.

The issues so far discussed related primarily to the ethics of research. Psychologists who deal with disturbed people must also follow ethical guidelines in forming judgments about applying clinical techniques. Recall the work that Wolf, Risley, and Mees did with Dicky. They brought certain aspects of his behavior under their control by shaping his responding much as we do with animals in the laboratory. In fact, these psychologists went so far as to deprive the boy of food! You may have wondered if such operations are ethical. Consider the situation. These men faced a decision. Dicky would lose his vision. They had to do something to help him. But what? They knew that food deprivation is a potent source of motivation. But taking food away from a child is a drastic invasion into his life. They had to decide which was worse for Dicky, going blind or going hungry. Dicky had nothing to say about it. They had to make an ethical as well as a clinical judgment. Going hungry for a short period of time obviously was a very small price for Dicky to have paid for his vision. However, the ethical questions that therapists face are not always so easily decided.

The work with Dicky exemplifies a broad ethical issue which every psychologist who actively intervenes in the life of another human being must face. He must ask himself the question: Do I have the *right* to change this person's behavior, or (perhaps even more to the point) Is the behavior I want to substitute for the maladaptive behavior really better?

The present discussion has only scratched the surface regarding ethical issues in research and clinical practice. There are many others which we have failed to touch upon. For example, do personality tests represent an invasion of privacy? Are there some operations we should not perform even with the consent of adult subjects? While these issues are important, they are beyond the scope of this text. We hope, however, that the above discussion has shown the reader that psychologists are deeply concerned with ethical issues.

CONSIDERATIONS WHICH MAY DETERMINE FUTURE QUESTIONS

We have gone to great lengths to demonstrate how questions must be made smaller and smaller in order to be made answerable. The reader may have been made uncomfortable by this argument, for it may well have seemed that the questions which were finally answered by the research bore little or no resemblance to the original question of interest, or perhaps to any question of interest at all. What do we do with the answers? Do we ever get back to the original question? Some psychologists believe that we will eventually answer these large, significant questions by formulating a comprehensive theory or, more likely, several relatively comprehensive theories. What is needed, from this point of view, is more data. That might be one way of ending this book, a call for more data, but again that would leave the reader with a false sense of the maturity of psychology as a scientific discipline. As we will try to show you, the situation is not so simple as the call for data implies. If we are not yet at the point in the development of psychology when we can put our answers to answerable questions together in order to answer "important" questions, what sorts of considerations will enter into the asking of future questions? As we said earlier, we cannot write down rules of thumb for asking good, answerable questions—good in the sense that they will ultimately lead to answers to the big questions. What we can do, however, is to describe some of the considerations which we believe will be extremely significant in determining the kinds of questions that psychologists will be asking in the foreseeable future.

We have already indicated that behavior is terribly complex. We will develop that point further. We will discuss the *interrelatedness* of questions, an interrelatedness which has led psychologists to attempt to develop progressively less comprehensive theories. And, assuming that the reader may ask why we try to theorize at all, we will give some of the reasons for theory construction. Also, we will attempt to present the position of those psychologists who challenge this traditional approach to the understanding of behavior.

Let us now deal with these issues in some detail, beginning with the question of interrelatedness.

INTERRELATEDNESS OF QUESTIONS. We have repeatedly indicated that there are numerous interesting and important questions which nonresearchers ask, but which are unanswerable. There are, in addition, many questions which, although couched in scientific-sounding terms, are also unanswerable. For example: What is the relationship between learning and perception? Does motivation affect learning? Does motivation affect perception? Does perception affect motivation? Does frustration necessarily lead to aggression? How do parental attitudes affect the later adult personality of a child?

The list could go on and on, but there is a significant point to be made. There are many reasons why such questions cannot be answered scientifically, many of which were discussed in Parts I and II. But there is yet another difficulty with these questions, a difficulty which may not be so apparent.

The complete scientific answer to any one of these grand questions about behavior is dependent upon our having complete answers to every other grand question about behavior.

In addition to all of the problems of answerability raised earlier, that is, those problems dealt with by reducing the question to manageable proportions, we also have the problem of the interrelatedness of the questions prior to any reductions. This interrelatedness has been implicitly recognized by every investigator cited in Part II. They chose to hold constant *all possible* influences on behavior except the one under investigation. Recall our discussion of control. Why did the various investigators go to such extreme pains to hold constant all extraneous influences? Why did they take what may have seemed to be such elaborate precautions? These precautions are eloquent testimony to the fact that these investigators are aware of all of the things which *may*, and *do*, affect behavior. One cannot study everything at the same time. So what the researcher does is to choose to ignore a large number of things which he knows *would* affect the results. He ignores them by holding them constant. But ignoring them in an experiment does not make them any less influential in real life, and holding them constant *in an experiment* does not mean that they are constant in real life. In fact, the various influences on behavior are all mutually interdependent—the effect of one depends very heavily on all the others. For example, when an investigator chooses to study learning and he selects adults as subjects, it is not because he believes that developmental considerations are irrelevant. It is because he can only study so much at a given time. The fact that he holds the developmental level constant does not mean that it is unimportant. It means that the investigator does not get any information about developmental influence, or about the relation between development and learning. What he does get is some information about the learning process in adults.

We began with a question about stress and personality. But you may well have noticed that the studies which we selected to present in Part II dealt with diverse topics: developmental and social psychology, psychosomatic illness, learning, perception, behavior pathology and its treatment, etc. It may seem that this was possible only because the construct *personality* refers to the whole person, but, in fact, the same could have been done for every one of the grand questions we posed. Consider what would be involved in establishing the relationship between motivation and learning. In order to investigate the problem scientifically, we would have to take all of the steps involved in reducing this to answerable questions. But we also face the problem just raised in this section. In order to understand an individual's motivation we must understand how the individual perceives the motivating situation. In order to understand the individual's perceptual process, we must understand his past history, which requires an understanding of the developmental process, attention, learning, and memory. All of this implies an understanding of individual differences, as determined by biological and physiological considerations as they have interacted with the past history of the person. Thus, as the relationship between motivation and learning, for example, may well differ from individual to individual, any complete theory must deal with the problem of *individual differences*. This requires an understanding of various forms of abnormal behavior as well as of various forms of normal functioning. This list, too, could go on and on. But the point has been made. The *complete*, scientific answer to any general question about behavior necessitates the *complete*, scientific answer to every other general question.

At the very outset of this book it was stated that virtually all "psychologists have abandoned the pursuit of the Holy Grail of grand behavior theory." At least they have abandoned this pursuit to the extent that they are not *now* trying to construct such theories with the data at hand, nor are they trying to generate the data which will lead to such a grand theory in the foreseeable future. Everything you have read between the two writings of that phrase contributes to an explanation of why this pursuit has been abandoned. An investigator who wishes to provide a complete answer to a grand question about behavior is faced with the formidable task of reducing his question to a large number of answerable questions. He is also faced with the presently impossible task of understanding all *related* aspects of behavior, that is, *all of behavior*.

This explains why many psychologists are trying to construct much, *much,* smaller theories, covering only a very limited range of behavior and environmental conditions, and often applying to but a single species. For example, some psychologists are trying to construct theories to explain how retarded children learn to discriminate between different but similar stimuli. Others are attempting to build miniature theories to explain color perception, that is, to answer the question of how many and what kinds of color receptors must be postulated to account for the facts of color perception and color blindness. There are miniature theories of hearing that are attempts to describe the processes by which sound waves are converted to nerve impulses. There are many other such limited theories, theories of speech perception, short-term memory, self-perception, dreaming, and so forth.

The construction of such a miniature theory may be possible in the lifetime of a psychologist interested in these phenomena only because he has deliberately reduced its generality and does not consider a wide range of other phenomena. In his experiments he controls these extraneous phenomena, keeps them constant, and prevents them from having an effect.

Some psychologists strive for the development of good miniature theories in the anticipation that some time in the future their limited theories will be integral parts of more comprehensive theories. Other psychologists pursue the goal of good miniature theories out of a conviction that the limited area of which they are trying to make theoretical sense is in and of itself important. They believe that their efforts will contribute significantly to the understanding of behavior.

WHY THEORY? At this point, or perhaps earlier, the reader may have wondered "but why theory?" If a comprehensive theory of behavior is as difficult a task as we have implied, then why should we bother theorizing at all? The response to that question is very complex.

Partially the answer lies in the history of science. By applying scientific theory the physical sciences have been remarkably successful in gaining control over many aspects of the physical environment. In general, scientific theory has proven to be one of the most powerful tools mankind has ever employed. In the past couple of centuries the application of the scientific method in fields like physics, chemistry, and agriculture has led to an astonishing improvement in man's *physical* environment. No comparable improvement has been forthcoming in our *social* environment, or in our understanding of behavior. Many psychologists believe that the success attained in other fields as a function of the development of scientific theory has demonstrated that such an approach is a profitable one for behavioral scientists to take. They argue that a good theory may be a very significant contribution to the understanding of behavior.

There is a second part of the answer to the question, Why theory? but before we can state it very meaningfully we will have to digress briefly to discuss the nature of scientific theory. The success to which we have referred has resulted in detailed analyses of the scientific method itself. The nature and function of scientific theory have been the objects of especially close scrutiny. Volumes have been written on this subject, but at a simple level of analysis there is considerable agreement.

Scientific theory is generally regarded as a means of ordering available knowledge about the universe. Theories essentially involve some broad assumptions (for example, man can be studied as a physical energy system), a set of interrelated constructs, such as we have discussed above, and rules for relating the assumptions and the constructs to observables. The goodness of a scientific theory depends in part upon the extent to which it orders knowledge. Frequently it is possible to construct two theories, of roughly equal simplicity, both of which explain the same set of data, the same experiments, the same body of knowledge. One of these theories may be rich in suggesting new hypotheses and new experiments, and may lead to a considerable amount of new knowledge. To the extent that it does this better than the alternative theory, it orders a wider variety of phenomena and thus is the better, more general, theory. There are other related measures of the goodness of a scientific theory. One of these was implied a few sentences above with the expression, "of roughly equal simplicity." That is, a good theory should be parsimonious; it should order a large number of facts with relatively few assumptions and constructs. It should be constructed so that testable hypotheses can be logically deduced from the theory.

With this very brief discussion of the nature of theory concluded, we now wish to return to the question posed earlier: Why do psychologists theorize?

The second part of the answer to that question really reflects the psychology of the psychologist-researcher-theorist and other scientific investigators. There is an intrinsic reward involved in constructing a good theory, even a very limited one. When the theorist weaves together his ideas in such a way that he can now integrate a set of facts that had previously seemed unrelated, and can predict new facts which had previously been unpredicted, he has achieved great personal satisfaction, as well as made a significant step forward in the advancement of the science. There is, as we suggested at the end of Part I in discussing why scientists do research, a great sense of excitement and the exhilaration of discovery—at least for the successful theorist. And the process is a self-replenishing, self-sustaining one. The data of new investigations require modification of the theory, and perhaps open up novel lines of research, requiring yet further modification. Certainly the satisfaction involved in creating a good theory cannot be communicated in print. It comes from many sources, not the least of which is the experience of success in a task which one considers both difficult and important.

AN ALTERNATIVE POINT OF VIEW. But there are psychologists who say that theory construction is not the best approach to take. They argue that at this stage of development of the science, psychology is not ready for the construction of theories of behavior, at any level of generality. When some say, "psychology is not ready," what do they mean? They may mean that despite the great amount of research carried out in the past few years, psychologists simply have not amassed enough factual material about behavior to begin postulating broad theories. Why haven't we? There are at least two possible answers to this question. The first is that human behavior is tremendously complex and that we have not been at the job long enough. The reader can best appreciate this complexity by reflecting back to our discussion on the difficulties encountered in giving a *complete* answer to any question about behavior. Recall that *complete scientific answers* to any question about behavior really require complete answers to *all other questions*. The statement that a problem is complex does not, of course, mean that it is unresolvable. Human behavior may be no more complex than some of the problems physicists have faced in their efforts to understand the physical universe. However, it is true that psychologists have been at their scientific job for relatively fewer years.

But this is not the only answer to the question: Why haven't we amassed enough data? The second and more critical answer is that we may not have been exploring behavior in a fruitful manner. In fact, some may argue that not only have we been at the business of research for a short time but also that we have wasted a good deal of that time asking the wrong questions. Those psychologists who have been constructing theories have been trying to gain some understanding of behavior by postulating *constructs*—anxiety, emotion, arousal, fear, the unconscious, stress, personality. A very simple example of the theoretical approach in psychology might involve studying the construct *hunger drive*. We might deprive rats of food for twenty-four hours (the antecedent condition) and observe their running down an alley to eat (consequent behavior). We may then deprive rats for forty-eight hours and observe that they run even faster. How can this behavior be understood? One approach would be to infer the construct *hunger drive*, a drive which is unobservable in any direct sense but which, we postulate, intervenes between the number of hours of deprivation (the antecedent condition) and the speed of running (the consequent behavior). Once constructs are defined in the above sense, psychologists attempt to link them together in logical systems to form theories about behavior. It can be argued that a good deal of research time and energy has gone into studying behavior in an effort to clarify the nature of our constructs rather than studying behavior in an effort to understand and clarify that particular behavior. In fact, we must carry out many studies relating to a construct before that construct can be useful—before we can meaningfully employ it in attempts to order and predict behavior in a wide variety of settings. We must be able to *show* that by inferring a construct like conflict we are better able to understand and perhaps classify behaviors which may, on the surface, seem unrelated. No construct can be defined or made useful in the above sense by carrying out only one experiment.

Why do some psychologists argue that it is wrong to try to clarify constructs? Why should this be a problem? Why do some argue that these efforts have been a waste of time? Psychologists in the tradition of B. F. Skinner have argued that these constructs are not only unnecessary for our understanding of human behavior, but may actually *interfere* with such understanding. They argue that we don't need constructs and that we don't need all of these complex theories. If they are right, we don't need to carry out all of this research which focuses upon theory development and construct validation. But if one argues that the theoretical approach is not useful and meaningful, then it is incumbent upon him to suggest an alternative. The Skinnerians have. They argue that we can understand behavior through a careful analysis of the contingencies in the environment. By contingencies, these people are referring partly to the consequences of the response an organism makes. But this is not all. Skinner and his followers are also interested in the stimuli in the environment which control the response. Let us consider a concrete example in order to clarify these relationships.

Suppose we put a food-deprived pigeon in a chamber which contains a key that the bird can peck at. Also suppose that each time the animal does peck at the key he obtains a bit of food (that is, the consequences of the response are obtaining food). Soon we would have the bird shaped so that whenever we placed him in the apparatus given a certain number of hours of food deprivation, he would reliably peck at the key and eat. Getting food is *contingent* upon the pigeon's pecking the key. The result is that each time the pigeon pecks and receives food, the probability that he will peck again in the same situation is increased. Furthermore, we could then put a red light over the key and set up the apparatus such that no matter how many times the pigeon were to peck he would not receive food unless pecking occurred with the light on. Soon the pigeon would peck only during light-on periods. The red light has become one of the stimuli which control the response. As far as the Skinnerians are concerned, we now have everything necessary to understand the pigeon's behavior. We can predict the bird's behavior from a knowledge of the stimuli in his environment and a knowledge of his history in that environment. We can predict his behavior and we can control it. If he is deprived of food he will peck at the key when the red light is on. If we turn the red light off, he will stop pecking. We know this because we know what the environmental contingencies regarding pecking and receiving food have been, and we know what the relationships have been between the red light, the pecking responses, and the presentation of food. It is important that the Skinnerian be able to point to the relationship between antecedent conditions and consequent behaviors. The bird has been deprived. Pecking has led to food delivery. Is it necessary to know any more? Notice, no reference has been made to constructs. No assumptions have been made about what intervenes between the antecedent condition and the consequent behavior.

Within this framework the understanding of behavior simply refers to our being able to specify the probability that a response will occur. If you will think back to the section on Dicky you will recall that Wolf, Risley, and Mees were simply interested in shaping and controlling the boy's behavior by manipulating his environment, much as the pigeon's behavior in the chamber was shaped and controlled. No emotions or personality constructs were referred to.

The case of Dicky provides for us a good contrast between the highly theoretical approach to understanding behavior and the approach taken in the Skinnerian tradition. One could ask the question: How can we explain Dicky's tantrums? The theoretically oriented psychologists could well invoke a number of constructs to explain the behavior disturbances observed. One could argue that the boy's self-destructive behaviors were caused by hostility toward the parents. Or it could be argued that Dicky was suffering from strong feelings of rejection which were causing him to behave in ways which would call attention to himself. Similarly one could invoke concepts such as conflict or frustration to explain the tantrums and the glasses throwing. In fact, since Dicky suffered a severe visual impairment it could quite easily be argued that he was constantly frustrated since he could not clearly see and thus could not easily interpret the events in his environment. In fact, concepts like these are often used when psychologists attempt to diagnose or understand the behavior of others. But let us contrast this with the Skinnerian approach. Psychologists in this latter tradition take the position that these constructs are just not useful in predicting and controlling behavior. It is simply not necessary to postulate them. To Skinnerian psychologists the important facts have nothing to do with what's going on *inside* people. They would argue that all we need to do is specify the behavior we want to predict and control, determine the contingencies related to it, and change the behavior by manipulating those contingencies.

We do not wish to give the reader the impression that the differences between the theoretical approach and the Skinnerian tradition occur only in the area of clinical psychology. Skinnerians raise the very same objections to theoretical approaches taken in every area of psychological research. They object to explanations of the phenomena of learning, perception, and motivation, which rely on unobservables. In fact, if one takes the Skinnerian point of view one might argue that we have misused much of our effort in developing and investigating intervening, explanatory constructs. It is argued from this point of view that more progress would have been made in psychology had we spent our time studying functional relationships, that is, had we kept the goal in mind of systematically categorizing the relationships between antecedent conditions, behavior, and the consequences of that behavior.

WHICH APPROACH IS BETTER? You may have been impressed with the results with Dicky, and may also have been impressed by the argument above. If so you must be wondering why so much of this text has been devoted to the more theoretically oriented approach? Why have the authors taken so much time in Part I discussing constructs like stress and personality? And why has only one study in the Skinnerian tradition appeared in Part II? The answers to these questions are really quite simple.

Historically, psychologists have emphasized the theoretical approach. For years we have attempted to construct theories, to test them empirically, and to modify them as a result of our empirical tests. This approach has represented the mainstream of psychological activity. As such, there is a preponderance of work which has been aimed at clarifying and developing theories and constructs. Thus any attempt to represent psychological research and orientations to that research must reflect the activity in the field. Still, the reader could wonder if he is impressed by the Skinnerian approach, Why not forget all of this older tradition and focus on the newer approach? The fact is that it is not by any means clear if the Skinnerians do have "the answer." We do not yet know which of the two scientific paths contrasted above is the better. Skinner and his followers have raised some cogent criticisms of the theoretical approach. But there are many critics of the Skinnerian approach as well, and one cannot take their arguments lightly.

Recall that before Dicky was seen by Wolf, Risley, and Mees, he had been variously diagnosed as mentally defective and schizophrenic. Regardless of the label, it was generally agreed that Dicky had very severe problems in adjustment. Wolf, Risley, and Mees were able to *shape* certain behaviors and eliminate tantrums and glasses throwing, but they did not *cure* Dicky.

It is quite likely that psychologists would still consider Dicky's general adjustment to be abnormal even though he may now wear glasses and not have tantrums. While the gains made were important, they were also very restricted. For example, despite the fact that attempts were made to improve the boy's verbal behavior, Wolf, Risley, and Mees state: "his verbal behavior is by no means comparable to that of a normal five-year-old child" (p. 311). Outcomes like this are generally the case whenever the Skinnerian approach is applied to such severe behavior problems. Critics of this approach argue that just as only a small segment of Dicky's behavior was modified, so also this entire mode of attack, while successful, is drastically limited (DesLauriers and Carlson, 1969).

We can look at the problem in a more general sense. The Skinnerian approach can provide us with a way to analyze and control specific behaviors. However, many claim that it does not provide us with a system which is comprehensive enough to study many of the complex aspects of behavior that some think are crucial. Questions like, How does thinking develop? What are the relationships between how an individual perceives his environment and his own behavior? are ruled out in the Skinnerian system. Not only are they ruled out but the system does not provide a means for studying them. They are considered unimportant.

The argument goes back and forth, and research in both traditions continues at a rapid pace. Theoretically oriented psychologists ask and answer questions, developing, refining, and integrating their constructs. Skinnerians ask and answer questions, analyzing functional relationships and shaping behavior. But at this point in the development of psychology the question, Who is right? or Which is better? remains an unanswerable one.

CONCLUDING REMARKS. In the above section we presented two major approaches to the study of behavior. We have implied a two-category classification. Actually there are many, many scientific avenues open to the understanding of behavior. The two you have just read about are in some senses two ends of a continuum. These two share many things in common—and they share much in common with the avenues we have not discussed. Basically they all share a faith in and a use of the scientific method. Basically, they all share a belief that the kinds of questions which can most profitably be asked about behavior are those which can be answered by the scientific approach.

It is the authors' conviction that after seventy-five years or so of research our scientific knowledge of human behavior is extremely limited. But the reader must recall that men have been trying to understand behavior with nonscientific approaches for a much longer time. There is yet much to be learned about behavior. The search is exciting, and the discovery is exhilarating.

References

AMERICAN PSYCHOLOGICAL ASSOCIATION. *Casebook on ethical standards of psychologists.* Washington, D.C.: The Association, 1967.

APPLEY, M. H., & TRUMBULL, R. *Psychological stress.* New York: Appleton-Century-Crofts, 1967.

BAHNSEN, C. B. Emotional reactions to internally and externally derived threat of annihilation. In G. H. Grosser, H. Wechsler, & M. Greenblatt (Eds.), *The threat of impending disaster: Contributions to the psychology of stress.* Cambridge, Mass.: M.I.T. Press, 1964. Pp. 251–280.

BASOWITZ, H., PERSKY, H., KORCHIN, S. J., & GRINKER, R. R. *Anxiety and stress.* New York: McGraw-Hill, 1955.

BIDERMAN, A. D. Captivity lore and behavior in captivity. In G. H. Grosser, H. Wechsler, & M. Greenblatt (Eds.), *The threat of impending disaster: Contributions to the psychology of stress.* Cambridge, Mass.: M.I.T. Press, 1964. Pp. 223–250.

BRADY, J. V. Ulcers in "executive monkeys." *Scientific American,* 1958, *199,* 95–103.

CANNON, W. B. "Voodoo" death. *American Anthropologist,* 1942, *44,* 169–181. Quoted materials are reproduced by permission of the American Anthropological Association from the *American Anthropologist:* Vol. 44, 1942, p. 172.

DESLAURIERS, A. M., & CARLSON, C. F. *Your child is asleep: Early infantile autism.* Homewood, Ill.: Dorsey, 1969.

GRINKER, R. R., & SPIEGEL, J. *Men under stress.* Philadelphia: Blakiston, 1945.

HEBB, D. O. *The organization of behavior.* New York: Wiley, 1949.

HUNT, J. McV. The effects of infant feeding frustration upon adult hoarding behavior in the albino rat. *Journal of Abnormal and Social Psychology,* 1941, *36,* 338–360.

JOHNSON, H. J. Decision making, conflict, and physiological arousal. *Journal of Abnormal and Social Psychology,* 1963, *67,* 114–124.

KAHN, R. L., WOLFE, D. M., QUINN, R. P., & SNOEK, J. D. *Organizational stress.* New York: Wiley, 1964.

LAZARUS, R. S. A laboratory approach to the dynamics of psychological stress. In G. H. Grosser, H. Wechsler, & M. Greenblatt (Eds.), *The threat of impending disaster: Contributions to the psychology of stress.* Cambridge, Mass.: M.I.T. Press, 1964. Pp. 34–57.

LIDDELL, H. S. Conditioning and emotions. *Scientific American,* 1954, *190,* 48–57.

LIFTON, R. J. Psychological effects of the atomic bomb in Hiroshima: The theme of death. In G. H. Grosser, H. Wechsler, & M. Greenblatt (Eds.), *The threat of impending disaster: Contributions to the psychology of stress.* Cambridge, Mass.: M.I.T. Press, 1964. Pp. 152–193.

MASSERMAN, J. H. *Behavior and neuroses.* Chicago: University of Chicago Press, 1943.

MILLER, N. Fear as an acquirable drive. *Journal of Experimental Psychology,* 1948, *38,* 89–100.

RADLOFF, R., & HELMREICH, R. *Groups under stress: Psychological research in Sealab II.* New York: Appleton-Century-Crofts, 1968.

RAGUSA, D. M., SHEMBERG, K. M., & RASBURY, W. Escapable-inescapable shock and body weight loss. *Psychonomic Science,* 1968, *13,* 45–46.

RUFF, G. E., & KORCHIN, S. J. Psychological responses of the Mercury astronauts to stress. In G. H. Grosser, H. Wechsler, & M. Greenblatt (Eds.), *The threat of impending disaster: Contributions to the psychology of stress.* Cambridge, Mass.: M.I.T. Press, 1964. Pp. 197–207.

SARASON, S. B., DAVIDSON, K. S., LIGHTHALL, F. F., WAITE, R. R., & RUEBUSH, B. K. *Anxiety in elementary school children.* New Haven, Conn.: Yale University Press, 1960.

SCHACHTER, S. *The psychology of affiliation.* Stanford, Calif.: Stanford University Press, 1959. Quoted materials are reprinted with permission of the publisher from *The psychology of affiliation* by Stanley Schachter, Stanford: Stanford University Press, 1969. Pp. 13, 14, 15, and 21.

SEARS, R. R. Relation of early socialization experiences to aggression in middle childhood. *Journal of Abnormal and Social Psychology,* 1961, *63,* 466–492.

SELYE, H. *The stress of life.* New York: McGraw-Hill, 1956.

SHURLEY, J. T. Profound experimental sensory isolation. *American Journal of Psychiatry,* 1960, *117,* 539–545. Quoted materials are reprinted from the *American Journal of Psychiatry,* Volume 117, pages 539–545, 1960. Copyright 1960, the American Psychiatric Association, and the author.

SHURLEY, J. T. Hallucinations in sensory deprivation and sleep deprivation. In L. J. West (Ed.), *Hallucinations.* New York: Grune & Stratton, 1962. Pp. 87–91.

SKINNER, B. F. A case history in scientific method. In S. Koch (Ed.), *Psychology: A study of a science.* Vol. 2. New York: McGraw-Hill, 1959.

WOLF, M. M., RISLEY, T. R., & MEES, H. L. Application of operant conditioning procedures to the behavior problems of an autistic child. *Behaviour Research and Therapy,* 1964, *1,* 305–312. Quoted materials are reprinted with permission from M. M. Wolf, T. R. Risley, and H. L. Mees from *Behaviour Research and Therapy,* 1964, pp. 305, 306, 307, 308, and 310, Pergamon Press.

WOLPE, J. Some methods of behavior therapy. In C. Walker (Ed.), *Behavior theory and therapy in 1966.* Camarillo, Calif.: Camarillo State Hospital Psychology Department, 1966.